Achieve E-commerce Success with Volusion

Everything the user manual doesn't tell you about building an e-commerce business with Volusion.

Nick Choudry

www.codeaxa.com

Achieve E-commerce Success with Volusion

First published: December 2012

Published by Codeaxa.com.

Courage is not the absence of fear but knowing what to do in the presence of fear.

Who should read this book

Do you want to be shown, click by click the minutiae of how to set up a product or some other necessary but mundane feature? If so this book isn't for you.

If you want the hard facts, inspiration and secrets that don't turn up in any e-commerce book and wouldn't mind knowing were to find out about the mundane stuff as well. **This book is for you.**

Foreword by James Chiltern

When Nick asked me to write a few words to introduce him, I said I would on one condition. And I got his promise that he would stick to it.

The condition was that if I wrote a foreword he would use it, in it's entirety, unedited.

I have known Nick since 1998 and he's always had a spark for igniting something big, new or different. But in 2004, fairly early on in the small-medium business e-commerce rush, I noticed the spark become something more.

Certainly e-commerce was new and exciting, it still is relative to most other business models, but it wasn't just this that was getting Nick even more fired up than usual. So one day I managed to catch him with five minutes to spare. He explained to me something which I just hadn't thought about before, even though it had been staring me in the face for some years. Something which fundamentally altered all my medium and long term business goals, forever. Something really big. Not in a wealth creation sense but in the sense e-commerce could be used as a tool to define a new paradigm for how business, personal and family life coexist. And I know Nick is going to reveal all in the book, so I will leave you to discover it for yourself.

Needless to say Nick is a successful guy. Possibly his most impressive venture so far was PixelProtector. PixelProtector is a DVD which lets users get the best out of their HD TV. It was launched back in 2006 and has since sold more than a million copies across just about every country on the planet. And this was a back-room business where the only significant investment was Nicks time!

But his being successful, in my opinion, isn't Nicks most impressive quality. Success fades to almost insignificance when compared to Nicks drive to help *others* succeed. If you get a chance to speak to him he will probably try and dress up his selfless focus on other peoples potential, as some kind of selfishness, that other people succeeding helps him succeed. And of course, if your business is helping other businesses succeed then it is true. But that belies the real, genuine truth, that Nick cares about other people succeeding and if you get the chance of working with him I would definitely recommend it.

So if Nick is so great why did I make him promise what I did? Knowing that Nick is actually quite modest I wanted to find a way to guarantee that he would actually let me tell his readers the whole truth about him without him toning it down to protect his modesty.

Sorry Nick, you can stop blushing now and good luck with the book! Which chapter is the big secret in?

Message from Nick

Thanks James, I think. So why Volusion? First up I think Volusion is cool and there are a number of reasons for this. I will go into them in more detail in the book.

If you are of a similar inclination to the person described in the 'Who should read this book' section then there is a very good chance you will think it is cool too. And I urge you to investigate further.

If this book achieves just one thing, I want it to be a guide through the minefield of different e-commerce options available to the aspiring e-commerce entrepreneur, but I hope it will be much more than that.

I hope it will show you how to really boost your online store to the maximum level you dreamt it could be and perhaps a little higher. There are already hundreds of books that talk about business success and many thousands that will tell you which buttons to press in any given e-commerce software, but none that combine the two. Until now.

This book will explain why Volusion might be perfect for your business and then show you how to use it to the max, whether you do the work all yourself or call on my business, Codeaxa, for assistance at some points in your journey.

There is already a comprehensive support article database for Volusion that helps you with each and every button you or your team will need to press along the way. So this book, as the 'who should read this book' section indicated, isn't really about pressing buttons, although I will point out a few of the trickier or more important ones.

What this book is about, is the difference between an incredibly successful e-commerce business and one that does OK.

So here is to your incredible success! And if James is reading this it's in chapter 9!

Nick Choudry

www.codeaxa.com

Table of Contents

1

Succeeding in e-commerce

Some of the essential elements for succeeding in e-commerce are the same as are required for succeeding in any business. I am not, you will be pleased to hear, going to lecture you on the already well covered areas of managing staff, having a viable financial plan or any other such basics that you are most likely, already familiar with.

Neither is this chapter going to be anything to do with which buttons to press in Volusion, indeed this entire book has surprisingly little button pressing, considering the title implies it is about e-commerce software.

But that is just the point. If you want to know how to add a new widget to your widget store and set its price then there are plenty of sources of information that will quickly tell you how to do that.

As you are reading this I assume you are looking to build a professional e-commerce store that has turnover and profit to rival, if not exceed the equivalent bricks and mortar store. And this chapter will be going over in some detail all the things my experience has taught me are needed.

Some topics I will cover directly in this chapter others I will brush over and defer until later. I will also tell you where to get the button pressing information, or where to find someone to press the buttons for you, as and when it is required.

I believe you can nail down the essentials of a successful e-commerce business in four sentences. Here are the things your customers need and want that make up my e-commerce *paragraph of prosperity*.

Help to find a product they want

A product they want. That's a bit obvious? Well in a way it is. I am guessing that you already have a product range to sell, if not grab a copy of my last book, Wealth Creation Online it goes into detail about how to choose a range to sell online.

Of course having a great product range is essential but what I am talking about here is much more subtle. Read the title again. Help to find. Some newcomers to e-commerce think they can stick a website up and wait for people to buy their wares. The title 'Help to find' is relevant in several ways.

How do customers even find your site? They need help to find it. How do customers know which product is the right one for them? They need help to decide. Even when a potential customer knows a product is the 'right' one for them they only buy it when they 'feel' they actually want it. In chapter 4, I will explain how to help your customers find and decide what product is right for them by having a logical store layout and informative product descriptions.

So now your site makes sense to potential customers but how do they even find you? There are so many wrong ways to try and get your new business found. I will explain in Chapter 5, the right ways and, along with that, your choices of how to implement the right ways yourself or with hired help if that is more appropriate for you.

So you have a useful site and people are finding it. That's it right? Of course not, but you knew I would say that. They have to WANT to buy your product. You have to engage with them at an emotional level, not just a common sense/value for money level. How to write and present your products to make people want, I mean really want your products is not covered in any e-commerce guide that I have read and is considered something of a dark art by some. The truth is it is really quite simple when it is explained properly.

In Chapter 7: Volusion marketing. Winning your customers on all these levels are all part of the 'Help to find a product they want' stage of e-commerce. Moving on.

Presented stunningly

This the easiest part to explain but one of the most difficult to actually implement. Right back to when human civilization was still dragging it's knuckles along the cave floor, our species has been obsessed with appearance.

We choose who to breed with, who to trust (more soon), who to like and of course; who we buy from based in a significant manner, upon appearance.

Now you might be shaking your head and insisting to yourself that others may be as shallow as I describe but not you. Don't beat yourself up about it we can't help it. It's instinctive, controlled by our subconscious and there is nothing that can be done about it.

It is true that we could give ourselves a range of options to choose from and sit down in a calm logical manner and make a decision deliberately excluding appearance as a factor. But that is not how life is and that is not how buying decisions are made. And even if you are deep and meaningful enough to make decisions entirely based on pure logic, I guarantee you almost every visitor to your web-site is not!

So lets face the reality. Your web-site must be functional, findable, useful, blah. But it is nothing and I mean absolutely NOTHING if it is not extraordinarily beautiful, gorgeous and stunning to behold as well!

When you visit a web-site that makes you think 'ahh', 'wow' or even 'phaw' you give it a few seconds longer to give you what you want. A few seconds, when all the other things we have talked about are in place too, is all you need.

Chapter 3 talks about how to get the sexiest most desirable and shop-able web-site.

Supported efficiently

Support covers everything from the moment a customer tries to buy right up until they die! Period.

Once the customer has made a decision to buy, is it a quick slide at a summery park through to parting with their money or do they have to run upstairs, guess which door to go through and then break it down, to give you the honor of taking their money?

This is possibly one of the biggest reasons for one of the biggest problems e-commerce businesses face - cart abandonment. Your customer simply has not got the energy or the patience to get through your checkout process and they dump their cart in your beautifully presented virtual isle and go and buy their stuff from someone who can be bothered to make it easy for them. This massive issue and others is squashed forever across a number of chapters.

Support also refers to keeping your customer informed and responding to their needs before delivery, after delivery and all the time they are using your product. Systems and practices need to be in place in order to achieve this without an unnecessarily high burden of time on you and your staff and at the same time as making your customer feel like you care; because you do, right?

Most web businesses including some of the well established ones get this wrong. CRM or customer relationship management is made into a walk in the park in chapter 4.

So what did I mean about right up until they die. Was I just being dramatic? Not at all. This book will talk allot about how to get customers. It can be hard work, it can even cost money. So once you have a customer it would be madness to let them go. You need to keep selling things to them. But not by bombarding them with unsolicited, untargeted product offers.

By supporting them with information, ideas and genuinely related offers. These concepts are covered across several chapters including, Chapter 6, Chapter 7 and Chapter 9.

By someone they like and trust

Remember a few pages back I said ' They have to WANT to buy your product'. I would like to restate myself with a different emphasis. They have to want to buy YOUR product.

There is nothing worse than giving someone everything they need to make a buying decision, only to have them shove off to buy it somewhere else. This happens all the time.

It is common for an enthusiastic, knowledgeable site to provide all the detailed information a customer needs and then the customer goes and buys from one of the big companies they have shopped with before.

It is such a regular occurrence, to do your research and then go and buy at the cheapest place we are comfortable shopping at.

So here I have introduced two problems with selling online.

Firstly creating trust and secondly price sensitivity. How do you create trust through a computer screen and how do you stop your potential clients from getting all the information from you and then running off to some bargain basement warehouse to make the purchase?

Actually fixing point one fixes the second as well. When a customer trusts you, really trusts you it takes a really big discount for them to risk going for the cheaper option. So if you can create this illusive trust and you have competitive but not necessarily low-margin prices you will beat the bargain basement every time.

Amazon is not the cheapest by a long way (although it used to be). Apple is not the cheapest and could never be so. Even Ebay sellers are rarely the cheapest these days. Not the successful and honest ones anyway. You do need to be highly competitive but you don't need to cut your margins to the bone.

So the problem remains. How to build trust, through a computer screen, in potentially seconds.

So what do we have to do? Certainly there are measures like money back guarantees, secure payments etc. But even more important than these. What is it.

Your brand is your trust. It must convey, confidence, reliability and integrity. Easy to explain but implementation- not quite so simple. How to overcome this seemingly insurmountable problem is part of chapter 3.

In a nutshell

So if we put the last few titles/sentences together into my paragraph of prosperity we can quite succinctly arrive at a formula for success in e-commerce. For a successful e-commerce business we simply need to give people:

'help to find a product they want, presented stunningly by someone they like and trust (that's you), and supported efficiently'.

Of course it is easy to rattle of a few requirements and a rudimentary explanation of their meaning. I wouldn't be doing my job if I didn't go further. In fact most people who start an e-commerce business probably have every intention of achieving these things anyway. So why are most e-commerce sites just dull uninspiring examples of commercial mediocrity? Or worse?

Good intentions and hard work are not enough and understanding how to achieve these things in a cost-effective way is not the subject of any book I have read. That is why I decided to write this one.

First up on my list to help you achieve the stated aim and my paragraph of prosperity, we will look at the toolset required.

With any business we need the tools of the trade. In e-commerce there is a sometimes bafflingly enormous array of options. All touted by an even more baffling range of vested interests.

I am referring to the shopping cart, the web-site, the interface between you and your customers and the wide array of services and support systems like communication, payment processing , marketing, CRM and product presentation; that need to be integrated into it.

If you are thinking that all sounds a bit technical relax and read the next chapter.

2

Volusion Gold

Why have I written a book about general e-commerce success and based it around Volusion? There are a lot of reasons and it is much simpler to explain some of the vast array of e-commerce software options and their differences.

You will then be able to see the circumstances when Volusion is right for you and when it might not be.

E-commerce software

E-commerce or shopping cart software is an enormous oversimplification of the tasks we ask these diverse bundles of computer code to perform for us. Most shopping cart programs do much more than provide a web-site for people to shop at and an interface for the web-site owners to manage the orders.

Shopping cart or e-commerce software is often used to describe software that does some or all of the following tasks. Stock control, CRM, payment processing, CMS, accounting, catalog management, site management, SEO, analytics/reporting, localization, internationalization, shipping handling, marketing(email/newsletter, product promotion), assisted shopping, social integration and the list goes on.

And it is not just a case of comparing features because some features can be implemented well in one solution and poorly in another.

Add to this the completely diverse nature of the types of solution. You might have heard of free shopping carts or open source.

Open Source

This is were a company provides a solution for free. I.e. the source (programming code) is open. Anybody with very few restrictions can download and use the computer code and use it as they see fit. There are many examples of open source shopping cart solutions but probably around half a dozen that are taken seriously by serious e-commerce businesses.

The advantage of these open source solutions is obviously the fact they are free. The disadvantages are less obvious until you have run a few different e-commerce businesses.

When a company gives you something for nothing it always comes with a nice long, but not so easy to understand disclaimer. The disclaimer explains the extent of the guarantee and their commitment to help your business succeed. And, unfortunately their guarantee and commitment is exactly what you paid for the shopping cart. Nothing!

Now it is still possible for one of these solutions to be the right choice for you. In fact I have written about them fairly extensively. If you are a hobby entrepreneur looking to spend next to nothing and you are highly skilled in PHP, Apache and JavaScript then there is an argument for considering one of the better open source options.

Now you might have been wondering why anybody in their right mind would set up a company making open source software in the first place? Open source can appear a very attractive proposition on the face of it. Many businesses go down this route. It is important to realize however that most of these solutions are not extensively featured and often end up with the need to purchase add-ons or extension modules for you to get the features you require. Modules that you have to work out how to install yourself!

Most who go down this route also end up contracting expensive programming and web server management professionals specifically skilled in the open source solution they chose.

Well guess what? The companies who made these solutions are more than happy to provide these services - at a cost. Services like this provided on a one to one basis will always cost more than a solution set up with the intention of supporting multiple customers from the outset.

Add to this the fact that even though the software is free you still need to physically put your web-site on somebody's web server. This is never free and all the major web hosting companies distance themselves from supporting or assisting with open source software. They are happy for their customers to use it, they just don't want anything to do with it when its not working.

Closed Source - semi bespoke

Software solutions you have to pay for. These are very expensive. Tens of thousands of pounds to get started. Some of the open source solutions have premium, closed source versions of their products. And guess what? You still need to setup and maintain things yourself. These solutions are good if you intend to very quickly be turning over six figures per month and you have an entire IT department at your disposal. If this is you then you should have read the bit at the start of my book titled 'Who this book is for'.

Bespoke

Multinationals only. Enough said. A warning. Many small and medium sized web design companies will offer you apparently bespoke systems. They rarely are and are usually re-branded open source solutions. And leave you in the worst of all worlds because you can find yourself tied to one company and if the relationship sours you may have to start from scratch.

Turnkey solutions

That's what I call the next category of shopping cart solutions. There are pros and cons to turnkey options as well. Here they are. This is were the same company supplies the software, support and hosting.

One downside to turnkey solutions is that typically they have a higher monthly cost compared to web hosting alone. Also a turnkey solution is provided in its specific managed-hosted environment so if you want to hire some programmers to implement something totally unique, then often you can't. So if you choose a turnkey solution you have to be sure it meets your needs now and in the future.

The potential advantages of a turnkey solution are numerous, but notice I said potential. Not all turnkey solutions are created equal.

One potential is the opportunity it gives the turnkey solution provider to give centralized and there for vastly reduced cost of support. If the underlying technology is the same across all its customers stores then a problem found in one store can be immediately fixed preventing the issue from ever being noticed in tens of thousands of other stores.

This advantage is, in a way, applicable to the open source solutions. If a bug or problem is found in an open source shopping cart then certainly the open source provider can fix the problem. The difference is that patches or reinstallations will need to be undertaken by each and every company who has one of their stores installed. The other comparison that favors the turnkey customer is that the turnkey provider has a serious vested interest in fixing the bug as fast as possible.

The other potential is to provide services which open source companies or bespoke providers can only dream of. Services like a content delivery network which makes a website apparently hosted in the UK appear at lightening speed in say the US. Providing this service to tens of thousands of customers makes it affordable to even a relatively small business.

Achieving this kind of service level when paying just for hosting would start to put the cost of the apparently cheaper open source options closer to some turnkey options but without the benefit the turnkey providers offer.

A turnkey solutions provider can use economies of scale to offer human support on a more accessible basis than even the small/medium web design company can. Let me explain. If the turnkey provider has tens of thousands of customers across multiple continents having someone qualified at the end of the phone becomes really affordable.

There are other benefits of scale which I will come to soon.

Why Volusion

Yeah why? I have investigated most of the turnkey solutions and Volusion offers all of the potential advantages I discuss above and implements them brilliantly.

Also their technology is so refined and evolved it is highly unlikely you will ever find a bug with their software. Ever.

Ease of use and support

Slightly harder to put into words is how, well, nice, Volusion is to use. The buttons are usually were you expect them and when you press them they tend to do what you expect.

But it would be a lie to describe Volusion as simple. The depth of features is comparable to the super high priced closed source system and there must inevitably be some complexity with some things.

But because Volusion uses their economies of scale so well there is someone at the end of the phone 24/7 to help you get what is critical to you, working, at the time it is convenient for you to do it.

There is the most comprehensive resource of manuals, guides and video tutorials that you could imagine and they are genuinely easy to follow.

Features

Here are a few of the things Volusion gets right that I haven't mentioned in detail yet.

CDN: Gives you a fast responsive web site in all the international markets that are important to you.

Extendibility

I mentioned as one of the downsides to turnkey solutions being that you can't hire programmers to implement your highly customized features. Well with Volusion you sort of can. The Volusion API enables third parties to produce a whole range of highly customized extensions enabling you to have completely unique functions.

This when you take advantage of Volusion's ability to use completely custom design templates and you have the best of all the solution types rolled into one.

So clearly this is going to be expensive?

Go for gold

Volusion offers five packages. One for hobby users with the Mini package right up to off the chart turnover businesses with the platinum package.

Have a look at: *http://www.volusion.co.uk/hosting-plans-pricing/*

Notice that the better the package the more features you get and of course, the higher the price. If you scan down the left at the features (more in a bit), you notice that for each increase in the package level you get a few more. This is until you get to the comparison between Gold and Platinum. Notice there is only one additional feature and yet a 20% increase in cost.

Unless you are really techno phobic you probably are not going to need the personal coach. You will have 24/7 phone support which from my experience is usually enough for any situation or emergency (of which there are very few with Volusion).

On the other hand if you look at the difference between Gold and the lesser packages you will notice fairly significant differences. Here is what the features of the Gold package give you in plain English.

You can have up to 5000 products in your catalog. If you have an even bigger range than this then it is one of the few good reasons to go for Platinum which offers unlimited products.

You get 15GB of data allowance. This is huge. You can build a massive turnover with this. There is one situation were this might not be enough and that is if you are showing lots of video from your site. But when we get to chapter 7, you will see how there is no need to host video yourself.

Volusion don't charge any transaction fees but this feature is not to be confused with the transaction fees you will of course be charged by your payment provider. It is worth shouting about this feature a bit because some turnkey solutions do attract transaction fees.

As we have already mentioned you get 24/7 support, with the Gold package this is on the phone.

Your store would be accessible from mobile phones and tablets, you could open a store on a Facebook business page (see chapter 8), you could, tweet on twitter, post to Facebook and manage your YouTube promo videos direct from your Volusion control panel.

You can track and manage those dreaded abandoned carts we alluded to previously, receive and manage ratings and reviews for all your 5000 products, run a newsletter marketing campaign, take orders over the phone, mange product or customer data in a tool you are familiar with, perhaps Excel and here comes a fairly important one. Use the excellent Volusion CRM (Customer Relationship Management) tools to help you fulfill the support part of the paragraph of prosperity.

You would have access to vital tools like deal of the day and MyRewards. These compliment the existing Volusion product marketing tools and allow you to really take advantage of cross selling, up-selling and related purchases at the same time as rewarding you customers for loyalty and encouraging return visits. More on this in chapter 7.

Now I am guilty here of simply brushing over some stunning features, some of which are even available in the cheaper packages. For example try and find an open source solution with an integrated mobile site. Let me help, don't bother.

Try and find a hosting provider who can offer the advantages of CDN (content delivery network) for the price of the gold package. It's not going to happen. You would need a dedicated server for twice the price and someone who can manage it for you.

These are some of the reasons why, when appealing to the serious e-commerce entrepreneurs I wrote a book about Volusion and not any other solution.

Oh, and in case you haven't noticed yet the price of the Gold package is under £100 per month. If you can't make your business work on Volusion it probably won't work on anything.

Codeaxa - That's me

So where do I come in, if at all? I have been working on Volusion for some time now. I have experts in every area of Volusion and can work with you to help you achieve every aspect of the paragraph of prosperity.

I will go into a bit more detail in the relevant chapters but Codeaxa and I can get your Volusion store up and trading, connected to your preferred payment gateways, catalog uploaded and make sure you know which buttons to press for when the orders start to roll in.

I can help you with whichever aspects of your Volusion business you like. I don't just get you started and disappear. More soon.

Where are we now

So you see- if you fit the description of who this book was written for then Volusion is almost certainly the best option for you, for the reasons I have alluded to.
You now have a great insight into the Volusion system we will be learning to exploit and hopefully the confidence that you are definitely going down

the right path to achieving your e-commerce goals.

It was the very same insight and confidence in Volusion that caused me to decide to specialize in, and write about it.

Right now you might be feeling some mild pangs of excitement that the realization of your business is getting nearer? When a path to a goal is revealed and it is a sure and well trodden path, it focuses the mind because the goal is more achievable than it was previously. So we now have access to these core tools of our trade. Lets nail down a few more essentials and maybe reveal a few more pathways at the same time.

3

Brand to please

We already know that a great brand can create trust. Obviously this trust has to be maintained and can't be abused or your brand will be the exact opposite, mistrust. But an appropriate, cohesive and directed message conveyed through the look, feel, logo, name, of/on your new website speaks louder than prices, promises of service or a small fortune spent on Google advertising.

But how can we achieve all these things?

1) The place to start is probably by deciding what it is you want to convey as your main message. Are you in the business of rapid service, big discounts, uniqueness, high quality?

2) Next think about specifically what you do. Not necessarily what you sell. More likely what can your customers achieve with your products. The wider your range the harder this will be because your ideas will be more generic.

3) Now think about what your stores mission is. Not it's mission to make you wealthy but it's other one. What does it intend to do for your customers?

4) Finally tailor your thoughts into a sentence that is worded and toned to the type of person you want to buy from you.

From these four questions you can start to derive two really important parts of your new branding. A tagline and a store name. Just because you are Company XYZ Ltd. doesn't mean that has to be the name of your web-site.

An example might help. I have a business that sells DVD's so people can calibrate their TV and prolong their life (the TV's not the customers).

A temptation might be to call the website TV-Calibration.com with perhaps a tagline like 'Calibrate your TV with Calibration.com'.

But the name and the message lacks any explanation about what the customer is really getting from the product and it has no depth with regard to the mission of the company and of course it has jargon, 'calibration' in it.

So the mission of the company is to give people a tool they will love using, feel good about owning that makes them feel like they are technically endowed but without being complicated.

What customers can actually achieve with the product is to look after their TV. But they can do that by refraining from hitting it. There must be something more specific. So I drilled down a little further. How does it look after the TV? It evens the intensity of the tiny dots of light which make up the picture in a modern TV. So it kind of protects the picture quality. The dots are known as pixels. Pixels is semi-technical but not geeky by any stretch of the imagination.

So I have examined the mission of the company what the product actually does for the customer all I have to do know is consider the overall message/impression I want to convey.

Technological, yet simple. That's the message. Here is the store name and tag line. You probably guessed already.

PixelProtector: Turn your DVD or Blu-Ray player into a high-tech setup and maintenance tool.

The important thing here is not the result I came up with but the process I used to get there. And obviously it should be apparent that I didn't mention the weeks of deliberation, trial and error and brainstorming of myself, friends, family and prospective clients.

The questions you have already asked yourself should also help you start to think about the colors and shapes, look and feel that you want to create on the site. Including how to incorporate a logo into it.

It is probably important that even if you are going to outsource your branding and design work that you should play a significant role in the process we have just discussed. However when it comes to the artistic part of wrapping your name, tagline, mission and benefit to the customer in colors, site design and logo, the process becomes somewhat less easy to convey in a book. But still, here are some ideas.

Look at other web-sites in your sector. Which of them appeal to you instantly? Without clicking on lots of pages and getting all analytical about it. A poorly implemented site, which on close inspection you decide is not a good example, might still have an initial warm and fuzzy feel about it. And that's what we are looking at now. Find at least a few and then analyze the colors shapes and images (excluding the products).

Look at the different styles and colors they use for fonts, borders and headings. Can you put your finger on what it is that you like about any of them? Write it down.

limexb360.co.uk

Look at how the limexb360.com logo, header, core colors and shapes all combine into one overarching feeling. The brand glows with excitement and the website just longs to be your coolest friend.

Sum of the parts

You now need to think about specific parts of your website. Expand your search to any e-commerce website at all.

Homepage

Start noting the different ways that the homepage is implemented. Do the sites that you like have loads of products on the home page, do they have dozens of different categories to choose from or is the homepage more abstract with a few large prominent category links and images? What do you think will work for YOUR customers? Write it down.

windscreenwipersdirect.co.uk

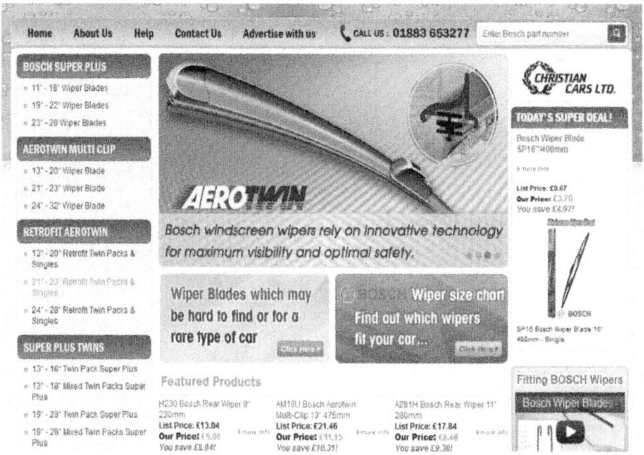

The header rotates to show multiple different messages. All the messages integrate perfectly. A balanced mix of offers, products and service promotion.

Category home pages

Now repeat the process for category home pages. That's the page which introduces a part of the range. For example on Amazon there is a Books home page. Ask yourself the same questions and write down your ideas. Obviously I don't know anything about your business so my questions might throw up some very specific reasons why your pages can't be like anything you have seen so far. That's good write it down.

dictaphones.co.uk

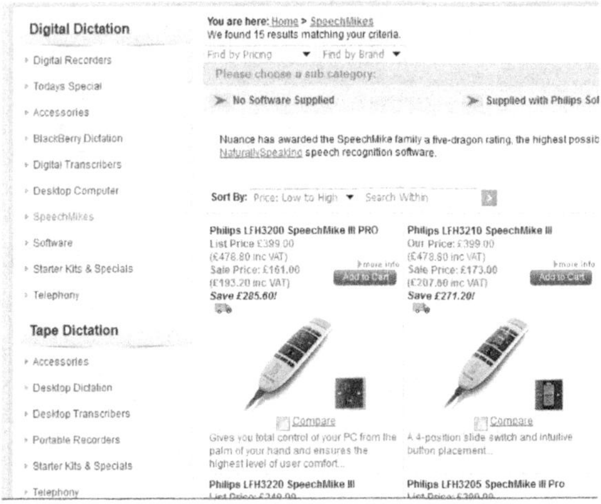

Brief and to the point category introduction, top category products, and further category refinement options on the left.

Template options

Here are your main options when choosing a template for your Volusion store.

Stock Volusion template

You have probably gathered from what we have talked about so far that this is not an option if you are serious about building a unique, credible, trusted and liked brand.

Volusion have done a great job on there stock templates and even offer a few customizations through the Volusion control panel but they are only really for businesses who are working on a tiny budget, hobbyists or where the shop-front is not the most important thing.

Independent designer

There are loads of great independent designers. And if you know where to look and how to tender you can get a really good deal. The problem with any great designer is they are usually just that. Great designers, but not Volusion specialists. And responsibility for integration of their work will often fall to the shop owner. Or, even worse, a sub standard implementation results.

Volusion specials

Volusion offer a premium template range but they still don't get anywhere near the complete integration and layout customization achieved by a bespoke design.

Volusion bespoke

Now we are getting there. Volusion themselves offer a bespoke service. This comes at a really significant price though.

The other potential issue is when you want a partial design refresh down the line you are not likely to get them to do it economically and that means handing their work over to an independent. And then your back to were you started.

Volusion deal with tens of thousands of shop owners and the economies of scale work really well for providing a great e-commerce environment but that scale doesn't in my opinion, translate so well when it comes to providing a unique, tailored experience which is what design and branding is all about.

Codeaxa

We are Volusion specialists and design specialists. We can create a brand or integrate/refresh your existing brand. All with Volusion compatibility and your specific requirements top of the list.

Logos, design of all parts of the store, color schemes, headers and banners all rolled into one stunning finish.

All the case studies are Codeaxa customers and you can see many more by visiting www.codeaxa.com.

Also we design with flexibility and refresh-ability in mind. So you can refresh significant parts of your site without spending more. (See chapter 6 about FTP for more details.) This means your store is kept stunning and new for longer, maintaining the goals of the design for longer and saving you money.

Why not fill out a design proposal for a free quote?

Where are we now?

Whichever route you take, if you focus intently on consistency of your message and have it implemented skillfully, you will have created trust and gone some way to being somebody your customers like too.

Chapter 4

Products & Selling

There are lots of ways you can help your customers to choose and buy. But what this chapter focuses on is the best form of help for both you and your customer. The kind of help that once you have done it once happens automatically every other time a customer visits and only needs tweaking and updating occasionally.

I am talking about helping your customers by making shopping at your store so easy that they can help themselves. Lets start with category design.

Category design

It is not complex or technical in any way but I have seen so many stores that don't appear to have thought it through properly and spoil an otherwise excellent shopping experience. So I thought I should run through some basics.

First lets clarify what we mean by categories. When you click on Books at Amazon that is a **category**. You are then offered a choice of Books,

Kindle Books, Books for Study and a few more. These are the **sub-categories**. There are also more choices when you click on the sub-categories, these reveal the **sub-sub-categories** and so on.

The purpose of this discussion is to end up with the best structure for your store.

Think about what you sell. Ok done that? Now think about what you might add to that range in the future. Now ask yourself what is the easiest way you could organize things from a customers point of view?

Think about the type and depth of your range and ask yourself these questions.

- Could my product range be considered as vast by my customers?
- Are the choices my customers make about which product they buy, based more on preference or specific need?

The questions above are designed to help you decide about the category and subcategory product arrangements. If you answered yes to both questions you will probably have a deep and wide arrangement of categories. If you answered no to both it will probably end up more flat and narrow, but in a good way.

An example. If you sell clothes, say, coats, jumpers, t-shirts, trousers, skirts. Well clearly a male customer is likely to err on the side of trousers rather than skirts so you might think to answer yes to question 2 but I would say that the need is so obvious that I would answer no because preference is the stronger argument, which color trousers, which style etc.

In this case I would be thinking about a flatter structure, unless I had hundreds of trousers (yes to question 1) then I would need to consider a way to subdivide the trouser range up.

On the other hand if you were an online plumbing and electrical parts store you would need a shallow top set of categories. Plumbing - Electrical. And then get quite deep and wide below that.

Don't be afraid to mix and match. Put appropriate products in more than one category or even whole sub-categories into more than one higher level category.

Now consider that perhaps you only have half a dozen or even less products. What then? Think about the different reasons a customer might buy your products and arrange them accordingly.

A good example is PixelProtector. There are only a few different disk types but the disks each achieve several different things for the customer.

Now each customer is likely visiting my site because of only one problem and therefore it makes perfect sense to name the categories after the problem/solution and pop the same range of products into each. Have a look at www.pixelprotector.com if you like.

The point is, you are not trying to compartmentalize your stock how you might like to see it- neat and tidy in a warehouse, you are trying to 'Help customers to find...'

My examples should not be the solution to your category planning just thought provoking enough to let you give some deep thought about the best, easiest, most enticing way to lay out your stuff. If your final solution is different to all your competitors, that is a good sign you have a better layout than they do!

Now you know your categories your design team can really get going with a design proposal for you. Contact me nick@codeaxa.com for a design requirements form.

Category descriptions

So many sites have dull category descriptions. They should clearly describe the category but not teach the customer to suck eggs and most importantly, they should sell.

Keep the descriptions short, probably a maximum of three or four paragraphs unless they genuinely need in depth descriptions to distinguish them from the other categories.

The category descriptions like your tag line should be a combination of fact and emotive description. What does this category of products do for your customer or what problem do the products solve.

If you have subcategories then the descriptions should get more specific with each level and don't let a category steal any thunder from it's more specific sub-category. And likewise, don't let any category or sub-category give all the juicy detail that should be in the product description. More on products in a while. The categories should entice and guide the customer to the product.

Adding categories in Volusion

Adding categories in Volusion is simple. Here is a really quick look. There is a more detailed guide in the Volusion knowledge base if you want clarification on any of the finer points.

In your Volusion control panel click on ***Inventory*** then select ***Categories***. Press the ***Add*** button, Name your category, type or copy/paste the description and any other details that are relevant to this category and press the big Orange Save button. That's it.

Now there were quite allot of options in the advanced section at the bottom. Don't worry about any of the search engine stuff for now. The rest just allows you to refine how the products are presented within the category. And the best way to do this will vary from design to design and can be discussed with your design team.

The Volusion 'Add Category' page.

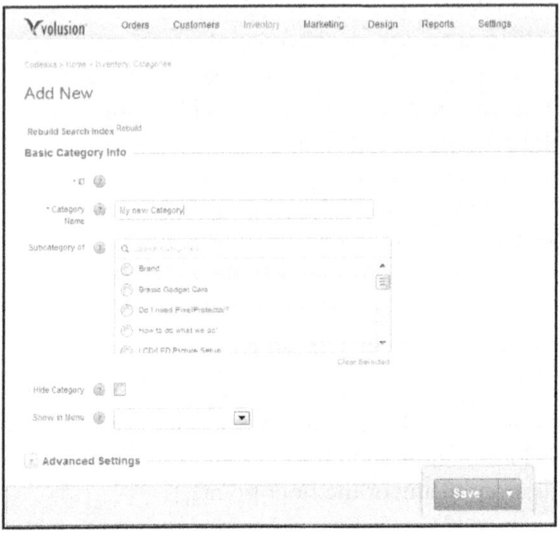

Product descriptions

As I have alluded to, the product descriptions are really significant to getting the sale. With that in mind lets talk about how to help your customer buy your products, a bit further. Selling and then closing the deal.

Adding products in Volusion

A quick glance at the add a product page in Volusion can be intimidating. There are many tabs and on most of the tabs a significant number of options and they are not all self explanatory. But creating really fantastic products can be done on just two of the tabs. Some of the other tabs are important as well but will be covered later when it is more appropriate. Examples of such tabs are the 'Search engine optimization' tab that will be covered in chapter 5 and the 'Shipping' tab that we will talk about later in this chapter.

Over the page is the most important tab.

The product descriptions tab in the advanced section

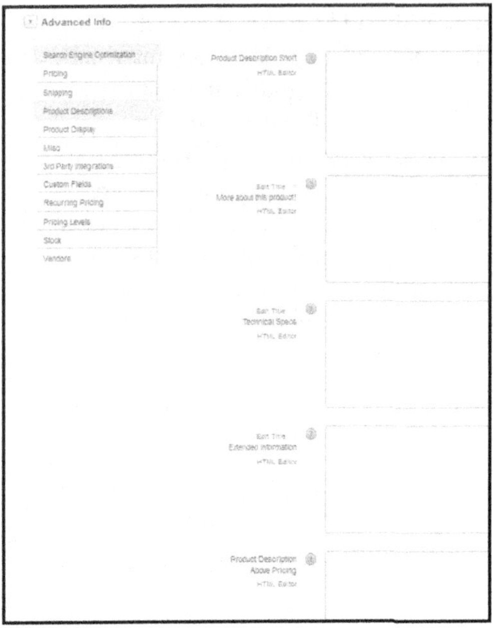

So you know what all the boxes are for thanks to the helpful Volusion pop-up links but I would tend to disagree with the example text given in the pop-ups. They tend to encourage slightly bland and simplistic content.

Here is a few tips on writing some interesting content to describe your products we can then look at into which boxes we might like to paste that information.

Writing to sell

Don't fall into the trap of simply describing your products. It might be true that a potential customer does need to know the dry facts like sizes and other uninspiring information, but don't put this information in the brief description or description boxes. Volusion provides places for bland facts—the 'More about this product', 'technical specs' and 'extended information' boxes.

The brief description and description boxes that will be described in more detail soon are there to sell to your customers—to increase their interest to a level that makes them "want" the product and then actually suggests they pop it in their cart and buy it.

The way you do this is with a very simple formula that actually works. And, of course, having whetted your appetite, it would be rude not to tell you about it.

Actually selling the product

Don't just tell your customers about your product, sell them the product. Explain to them why they should buy it! Use the FAB technique—feature, advantage, benefit:

Tell the customer about a feature:

- Nike bekams were designed by Nikes pro-dev team at the international sports institute in New York.
- This laptop has the brand new i7 processor made by Intel.
- This guide was written by somebody who has climbed Everest.

And the advantage that feature gives them:

- ...Making these the trainers that are the choice of professional athletes the world over.
- i7 is the very first processor series with a DDR3 integrated memory controller!
- So all the information and advice is real and has been actually tested!

Then emphasize the real emotive benefit this gives them:

- So you can look like the pro's and perform like them too.
- ...Meaning that this laptop gives your applications, up to a 30 percent performance boost over every other processor series ever made.
- Giving you the critical and most up-to-date information you need to purchase the right equipment for your expedition.

Don't just stop at one feature. Highlight the most important features. By most important features, of course I mean the features that lead to the best most emotive and personal benefits. Not too many though. If your product has loads of benefits, then try and pick just the best ones.

Three is perfect. Three really is a magic number. All the best things come in threes and scientific research actually proves that thoughts or ideas presented in threes influence human emotion the most. If you must have more than three features, summarize them in a quick bulleted list. Three is always best though.

- Soft, strong, and very long.
- Peace, love, and understanding.
- We came, we saw, we kicked its a**.

Ask for the sale

When you have used the FAB technique, ask the customer to part with their money!

- Say something like, "Select the most suitable option for you and click on Add to cart" or:
- "Remember that abc is the only xyz with benefit 1, benefit 2, and benefit 3. Order yours now!"

Whoops- Only 2 examples there. You get the idea though.

Where to put all your hot content

Paste the full version of your product 'description' in the description box. A shortened version in the 'product description short' box. Notice that below this there are boxes for other types of description as well. These are the places you can add the slightly blander informational descriptions.

Images

These have to be stunning. Get a pro to do it if you can. Here are a few tips if your doing it yourself.

Photograph the product as you would see it on the shelf/peg etc. What I mean by this is if for example,

if the Nike bekams come in a presentation box then this is how you should present it to your customer (initially). It is true that the customer might also want a close up of the lace holes or the logo, but the main, most important shot should be of the product as it would be on the store shelf.

This is the format the most successful retailers use.

Product delivery options

Setting up product delivery options is probably one of the most technical parts of any new ecommerce store. Volusion has a ton of options, not because it is unwieldy by design but simply because it is necessary in order to accommodate all the possible requirements of different product types. Think about just a few for a moment. Do you price by weight, order value or distance? All three? Do you have options like express or tracked? How does that impact the other options. What about digitally downloaded goods, free delivery on a few products but not all. The potential complexity can grow.

There is a Volusion video or tutorial for every scenario as well as a really good introductory tutorial. Just make sure that any complexity or lack of clarity is hidden from your customer or they will abandon carts like, well, hot potatoes. Fill out our delivery configurations questionnaire and table for a free quote at www.codeaxa.com and we will do it for you.

CRM

Customer relationship management you may have guessed is all about the support element from my paragraph of prosperity. But as you will see in later chapters it is just as beneficial to your bottom line profit as well. Lets take a look at how to support your customers using the Volusion control panel.

I keep going on about the professional help and support that Volusion offers you. But what about the professional help and support you offer your customers?

What can an existing customer do when they have a problem? Volusion (the company) has a comprehensive ticket system that enables you to send out multiple requests for help and track the response from multiple departments. So does your store. Here is how you and your customers can use it.

So essentially your CRM system is a means for your customers to contact you but at the same time, give you much more control and tracking facilities.

First we need to configure your store to use the CRM system.

Configuring your CRM system

First up we need to define some departments. These CRM departments can be organized any way you like but are usually defined along departments that already exist within your business. The example I will use can easily be tailored to suit your business. I will use Sales and After-sales.

Click on ***Customers*** then ***CRM System***. Now click on the ***Manage Departments*** tab followed by ***Add***.

Add CRM department

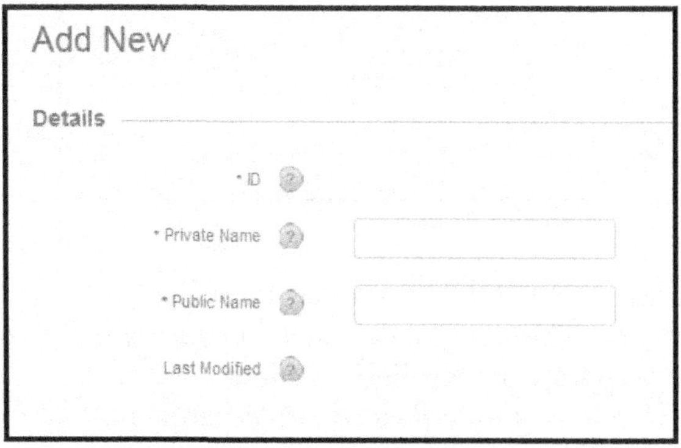

Filling this information out is simple. If you are using my departments you would simply put 'Sales' in the 'Public Name' box and the same in the 'Private Name' box. You have the option of naming the department differently internally to externally. If you want to do this then simply put a different internal name in the 'Private Name' box. Click Save at the bottom of the page and repeat until you have added all the departments you want.

Check out your new departments on the Manage departments page.

CRM Manage departments

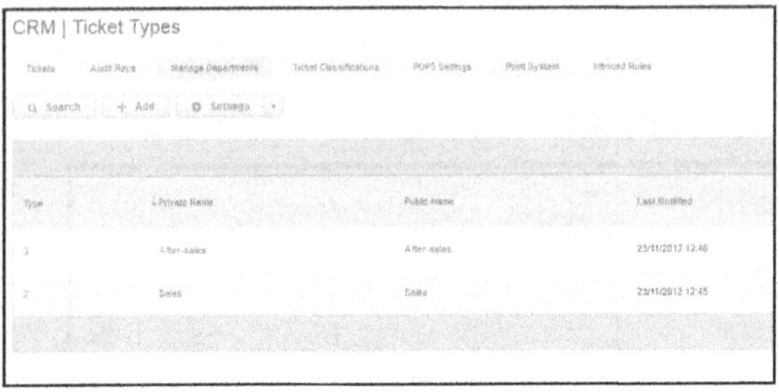

Now we want to create some classifications for our tickets. This is so we can filter enquiries we feel are appropriate for their question. Classifications are sub-divided into departments. So for example under the Sales department we might have 'Price enquiries' and perhaps a general 'More information' classification. And for After-sales we could have 'Where's my order' and 'Faulty product'.

If all these departments and classifications are getting a bit confusing then rest assured all will become clear when we start sending and handling tickets. For now think of classifications as the subject of the ticket.

Now lets create those classifications for the appropriate departments. Click on the ***Ticket classifications*** tab then the ***Add*** button. Take a look at the screen shot of what you will see. This is going to be really easy.

CRM Add classification

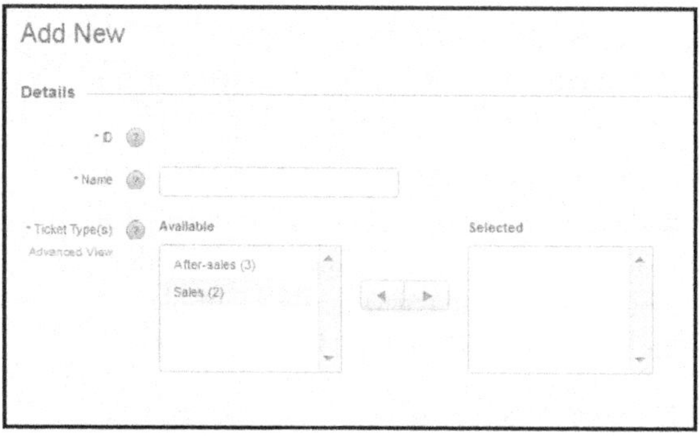

Type the name of your first classification in the 'Name' box.. In my case this is 'Price enquiries' in the 'Sales' department. So after typing the name I click the ***Sales*** *d*epartment then click the ***Right arrow*** so the department is selected. Now press ***Save*** and repeat for all your classifications. Note that the save button has a little drop down option where you can select 'Save and add new'. This is handy for creating lots of classifications quickly.

Connecting the CRM system

Now after all this configuration the CRM system still doesn't actually do anything. We need to connect it up to an email account and make sure the customers have the email address.

Setting up email

If you haven't already you need to setup a Volusion email account for each department. Even if you have already you might like to create new ones just to receive support tickets.

Here is how to do it. Log in to MyVolusion. On the left click on ***Manage Email***. Now click ***Add*** and fill out the box below. I used 'Sales' for the name as it matches the CRM department name. And don't forget to check the ***Active*** check box.

Add an email account

I then repeated the process and created another address called 'after-sales'.

Now we will connect your new support email addresses to your Volusion CRM system. Click on ***Customers*** then ***CRM System***. Now click the ***POP 3 Settings*** tab followed by the ***Add*** button. Here is the form we need to fill out. It is not as daunting as it might first look.

Connect email to CRM

For the ***Email*** and ***Email Username*** fields simply enter the first department email address that you want to configure. Now enter the same password you used when setting up the email address. And for the ***Email Server*** enter 'pop.email.srvr.com'. This is the address of the Volusion servers which handle their customers email. Select the CRM department that you want to connect to this email address in the ***Ticket Type*** drop down and we are nearly there.

The last 3 boxes are described below:

Email Reply Footer

This is the text that will be automatically appended to all the responses you send from the CRM system. You can put a company disclaimer, privacy statement or whatever you like here but it is probably a good idea to include a link to the ticket, so that the customer can click it from their email inbox and go directly to your site and view all the details and post a reply if necessary. Of course the link will be different for every ticket. Here is how you do it auto-magically. In this box type:

Your custom footer text.

To view ticket history, please visit: $(TicketURL)

Auto-Reply Subject

As the title suggests, when your customer creates or updates a ticket they will get an auto-reply from you, to reassure them you have received the message. What would you like as the subject of that auto-reply. Here is what Volusion suggest.

$(TicketNumber) Thank you for contacting us

The text '*$(TicketNumber)*' auto-magically puts in the relevant ticket number for you.

Auto-Reply Body

The actual message contained in the auto reply. Here is the Volusion suggestion complete with auto-magic link to the ticket on the Web.

To check the status of your ticket online, visit:
$(TicketURL)

Click ***Save*** and then configure POP3 for all the department/email address combinations that you need to.

Create link for customers

The only thing remaining before you and your customers can benefit from your new CRM system is a way for them to create new tickets.

The page which allows your customers to submit a ticket is:

https://www.yourdomain.com/Ticket_New.asp

Here it is:

ticket_New.asp

But we need to create an easy to find link to it. Lets put one in the customers account page. Then, when they are logged in they have an easy way to send you a message.

Sign in to your admin area. Now type in the address www.yourdomain.com/myaccount.asp replacing yourdomain.com with the address of your shop. Notice we are going about things a little differently to before. We are visiting a customer-facing page, but while signed in to our administrator account. This gives us more options.

Try this. Hover your cursor over the text at the top of the page and click ***edit***. You can add information into this field to add additional text and links to that area.

Here is a bit of sample code you could use. Customize it to suit you but this will create a brief message and a link so your customers can submit tickets. Copy/paste the following:

For post-sales help <a href=" /ticket_New.asp">click here </a>

then click ***apply***.

You can also add a link anywhere else on the site for the pre-sales questions. Now we have your links click on your links and create yourself a few fake tickets, sent to the right department and we will see how we can manage them.

Managing the tickets

Click on the Tickets tab of the CRM page. You might be left with something like this.

Managing the tickets

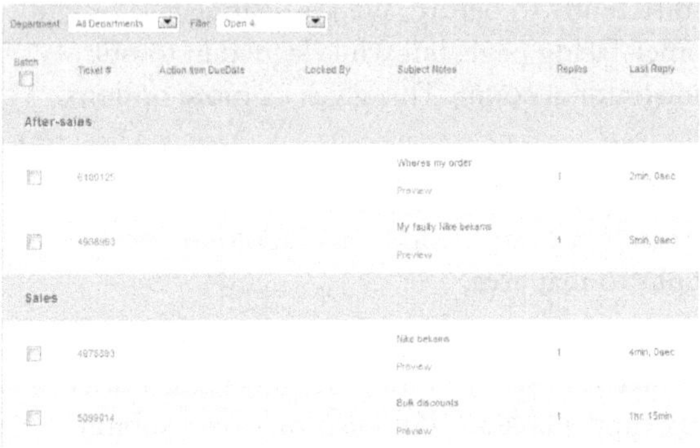

The first thing to note is the drop down's at the top that allow you to sort and order the tickets. Members of staff, if assigned different departments can view only their own.

Note the 'batch' drop down underneath the list of tickets that allows you to select multiple tickets simultaneously and then change their status.

You can also click on a tickets 'preview' link to see the message from the customer, before clicking the ticket number to manage the ticket. Try it now, you will see something like this.

A customer message

Click the ticket to manage it. Notice you can edit the classification. This is useful if your business has staff that deal with different types of query or just to classify things for your own clarity.

Of course, ultimately, the whole point of the CRM system is to keep in contact and respond to your customer. Type your reply in the box shown below and also notice you can type a private message for you and your staff, perhaps to remind you of circumstances affecting the reply that you don't want the customer to see.

CRM reply box

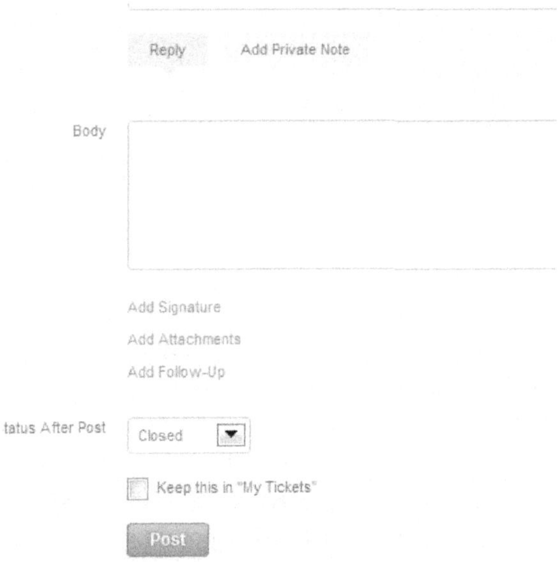

If you feel your response will end the matter, select the status as 'Close after post'.

Click ***post*** and your response will be sent whizzing through cyberspace.

Conclusion

Now you have a beautiful store, a fantastic product range, organized with your customers in mind and you know how to look after them. I guess we had better get some customers then.

5

Get Found

SEO or search engine optimization is sometimes considered something of a dark art. The truth is that real SEO is the exact opposite and improving your sites rank and the number of visitors you get for free is, like so many things in life, simply down to skill, planning and hard work.

Before we go on to examine the skills required, make a plan and start the work lets look at the biggest, potentially fatal mistake made by some aspiring e-commerce businesses and make sure we don't do the same thing.

If you've read somewhere of a way to boost your rank over night, get a ton of links to you in a hurry or get you on the first page of Google in a week? It is absolutely essential that you ignore it.

It is absolutely possible, (and its happened to me) that a new product or article will turn up top on Google, maybe for a really significant search term, but it won't be any scheme or quick fix that makes it happen.

Equally if an SEO consultant offers you remarkable results by the end of the day or even a week then don't believe them.

Google guidelines

Google themselves publish a list of guidelines which backs up what I'm saying and also warns that even *trying* to scam their system could result in being removed from their results entirely. And since Google still has around 90% market share, right or wrong, we have to play by their rules.

Tactics to definitely avoid include: Paid for links and volume swapping schemes. Never pay somebody else for a link. If their taking your money they are probably taking other peoples and they probably have or will end up with a junk rating with Google. And soon, so will you. Don't allow someone to setup websites on your behalf, just with the intention of linking to you. Certainly you might want a separate blog or some other related site and yes you can link to your e-commerce site. But keep the links to when they are relevant and keep the new content unique to the new sites.

Before moving on it is probably worth spending 10 minutes reading the advice from Google.

http://support.google.com/webmasters/bin/answer.py?hl=en&answer=35291

Measuring results

Before we move on to the right way to optimize your Volusion store we need to consider how we are going to know when we are doing things right and when we are making mistakes.

We can measure how we are doing using Google Analytics. Grab yourself a free account (just search for Analytics on Google) if you don't have one already and add your new site in your Analytics control panel.

You will then need to add a little bit of JavaScript code to your website. This isn't as daunting as it sounds and a step by step guide can be found here:

http://support.volusion.com/article/setting-google-analytics-volusion

Researching keywords and phrases

So we know not to do anything daft and we know how we will track our progress. Next we need to make some decisions. We need to decide which keywords and phrases we will optimize for. It might not be as obvious as you think. A case study might help.

Let's take a men's clothing store, as we briefly did in the last chapter. It sells trousers, shirts, coats and shoes. Which words should we be including and optimizing for in our content?

Well the obvious answer is trousers, shirts, coats and shoes. And that is true. But do a search for any of those items and you will see the first page and subsequent pages dominated by the big brands. It's going to take a long time to get up there. Probably years. Well that's fine let them keep there first page positions. For now.

If you were looking to buy a pair of shoes would you type 'Shoes'? Maybe but more likely you would start with something more specific like 'buy training shoes'. Perhaps because you know that most likely you will finally decide on a pair of trainers.

So now we know that we need to create content both for the general and the more specific. But that's not the end of the matter. We need to get more specific still. Jargon in the SEO business for this type of phrase is, long tail keyword. This is because it has the highly general, almost impossible to rank for word (shoes for example) at its head and a long tail of further, more achievable keywords as a tail.

Now the good news. Actually one more example first. You have just done your search for 'training shoes', checked out a few stores, probably the big brands, and come to the conclusion you want a pair of Nike bekams in red. Your a size 12. What is the average guy who wants these shoes going to search for next. Obviously it will be something along the lines of, ' Nike bekams red size 12 best price'. These long tail phrases are much easier to achieve coverage for. And it is your expertise in your industry which allows you to focus on the products and their associated long tail keywords in a way and with an intensity that the big brands cannot.

Oh yes, the good news. The person typing in a general keyword is probably only a little interested in viewing products related to this word. The more specific search indicates greater interest and the last long tail example means they probably have their credit card on the desk, itching to find a great price at a store they like and feel they can trust. Yours.

So to round up the choosing keywords section, we need to include and optimize for general, more specific and long tail keywords with the emphasis on long tail. How can we possibly plan such complexity. Well actually you already have.

By creating an elegant, logical and useful structure of categories, sub-categories and products, Volusion is ready and waiting for you.

The product pages will have long tail keywords, the category pages less specific and the home page the more general. Now you do have to include some long tails on the home and category pages as well, you also have to keep them optimized and change them based on your industries trends and your companies goals but here is how to get started. If you need help choosing the actual keywords, general, specific or long tail, Codeaxa can help. But when you have decided what the keywords and phrases should be, where do you put them?

What you write

Simple. Everything you write. Homepage blurb, category homepage and sub-category descriptions, product descriptions, articles (see chapter 7) and any other page on your site.

What about keyword density? This is easy as well. Don't stuff extra keywords in for the sake of it. Use as many and only as many as is natural to do when writing for a human. Chapter 8 expands on this with regard to writing articles and chapter 4 with regard to product descriptions.

Were else then?

Meta-tag, titles, descriptions and keywords

These are words and phrases that need to be crafted to fit your site but are not actually the words that your website visitors will actually read. With one exception.

Meta-tag titles are the titles some search engines will use to help index the title of your page. So they need to be highly relevant to the page.

Meta-tag descriptions amount to a summary of the contents of your page and are used by search engines to present a summary of the page in the search results they provide users. So as well as containing the appropriate keywords and phrases they should be enticing to improve the number of times the link from search results is clicked.

Meta-tags keywords. These are not used by many search engines but they are still part of the make-up of a well formed web page and therefore should be utilized.

Here is what to do about all these meta thingies. Volusion has a very convenient set of tools were you can simply enter your meta-tags. The product pages are on the same page as where you create the product, the category/sub-category meta-tags can be entered from the same page where you created the category details. And for all the other pages there is a special dedicated SEO page. So:

To create product meta-tags.

Click on ***Inventory*** and then ***Products***. Choose the first product and scroll down to the advanced section. Click the ***Advanced Info*** dropdown and the boxes to enter your meta tags are revealed.

To create category/sub-category meta tags.

Click on ***Inventory*** and then ***Categories***. Choose the first category and scroll down to the advanced section. Click the ***Advanced Info*** dropdown and the boxes to enter your meta tags are revealed.

To create all the other meta-tags.

Click on ***Marketing*** and then ***SEO***. All the pages are listed on the left and all the boxes to enter your meta tags are on the right.

In case your reading this before you have your Volusion store this is what the meta-tag entry pages look like.

Product page meta-tags

Anchor text

What's this and were does it go. It is a link containing keywords that links from one page to another relevant page. Volusion creates many of these for you in the form of links to products from category pages.

You can create more of them in the product, category and any other page you create. A great place for anchor text is within your articles. More in chapter 7.

Inbound links

As the name suggests these are links from other sites to your site. We have already talked about fake links and that is not what this is about. But inbound links from sites regarded as an authority in your industry and even better which ranks highly for the keywords/phrases you are targeting.

You can get and place links like these on relevant forums and other sites. This type of work is called link building and the technical term when you are successful at it is called building authority. It is potentially more significant than all the other forms of SEO put together.

Doing this properly takes time, effort and skill.

Blog and CMS

I will go into these things and how to do them properly in the marketing chapter. Just know for now they can be a very big part of search engine optimization.

The SEO toolkit

Just as Volusion is your e-commerce toolkit there are a number of tools specifically very good for your SEO efforts. There all free. Here they are along with a summary of what you can do with them.

Webmaster tools

Type in Webmaster Tools on Google and sign up for this free service. It gives you so much for nothing.

- Get notifications of errors on your pages.
- Find out which words your site is ranking for.
- Submit site maps.
- See Google data about when it crawled your site.
- And more.

You cannot do without this tool.

Adwords

Google Adwords is the paid adverts you see at the top and down the side of search results as well as the Google themed adverts you see on some web sites. Advertising with Google is covered in chapter 8 but what is relevant to this SEO discussion is that if you sign up for an Adwords account you can use the free Keyword tool to help you identify the volumes which people are using to search for keywords. This is invaluable to help you decide what to optimize for.

Analytics

Already mentioned in the beginning of this chapter you should be set up to start receiving Analytics data. Log in and study the sheer depth and variety of statistics to help you monitor your or your SEO professionals results.

Hiring SEO professionals

Bad SEO is known as black hat, like the baddies in the old cowboy movies would often wear black hats. Unsurprisingly high quality, non-risky SEO is called white hat.

So how do you know if the person you are hiring is white hat. Just ask questions. Ask for a breakdown of the activities they will undertake for their fee. If it doesn't include all of the areas we discussed then they probably lack experience. If they include any areas we now know as black hat then they are not reputable.

A more subtle indication of their knowledge and intention is to ask for the duration of their work. If they ask for a huge upfront fee for a relatively brief amount of work then chances are they are not what you want. The reason for this is that SEO is very much an ongoing process. It involves lots of small changes over a longer period of time.

The other aspect to look out for is the setup of the company you choose. It takes enormous skill to find and select keywords and phrases and this process should involve extensive consultation with you, unless they just happen to be expert in your business too. Although this is not likely.

On the other hand filling out your meta-tags, once the keyword scheme has been devised, although not entirely trivial does not require a highly paid consultant. And the skills required to write great (optimized) articles is far removed from that of keyword research.

Somebody you trust to have access to your analytics data is also essential so somebody who introduces themselves through un-solicited email is unlikely to fit the bill either.

Codeaxa has a range of levels of consultants and writers to perform the highly skilled, semi-skilled and creative work as well as efficient data entry staff to do the many hours of keyboard bashing.

And I hope if we speak in person you will learn that you can trust that your Analytics data will be safe in our hands as well.

6

Help is at hand

You are absolutely guaranteed to get stuck from time to time. I am not talking here about the really big challenges were you expect to spend time and money. If designing your store or devising your SEO strategy causes you a few headaches and takes a while then it is easy to take in your stride because you know they are tough to get right.

But when some damned stupid annoying button doesn't do what it is supposed to or the button isn't there or you don't even know where the button is supposed to be! These are the types of problems that annoy the hell out of me when they stall my progress and cost me serious time and money. Because they damn well shouldn't. These are the types of problem were you shouldn't need to pay someone to fix them. And, of course with Volusion, you don't.

Your first port of call when these events occur should be the Volusion knowledge base. Not because I want to save Volusion staff time but because the knowledge base is very easily searchable, has almost every answer you will ever need. So it saves you time.

If you haven't found it already it's time to login to MyVolusion.

My Volusion

When you signed up for Volusion you will have received a link, username and password. Click it and login now.

Here is what you will see. Any tickets you have posted requesting help. Here's some I made earlier. And down the left is links to all the different areas of MyVolusion.

MyVolusion home

My Resources

Knowledge base is the first link here. I think I have said it before but the amount of information here is unreal. Have you ever opened a manual to find it doesn't cover what you need? That has never happened to me with the Volusion knowledge base. Click on it to see what you get.

Quite extensive I am sure you will agree. Generally speaking however it is not always easy to guess correctly which topic contains the specific nugget of information you are after. I usually find myself doing a quick search.

Lets pick something obscure. Suppose you have setup your mobile template and you want to make it easy for customers with Android phones to shop with you. You need to install Google Wallet support for your Volusion store as it is the payment method of choice for millions of Android users.

Lets type 'setup Google Wallet'. Voila!

Knowledge base search results

Support home Build my store Manage my store Expand my store Contact u

Search Support: setting up google wallet

Support Home › Search › setup google wallet ›

Search results

Setting up Google Wallet

Google Wallet shipping methods as needed by repeating these steps. The **setup** process for **Google** ... **Google Wallet** - formerly known as **Google** Checkout - is **Google's** electronic payment service, similar to PayPal. Integration is done online and is easy to configure. Note that **Google Wallet** currently ...

Knowledge Base Article

And then just click and we have an easy to follow guide on how to get Google Wallet customers supported in around about 10 minutes.

Step by step guide installing Google Wallet

Setting up Google Wallet

Google Wallet - formerly known as Google Checkout - is Google's electronic payment service, similar to PayPal. Integration is done online and is easy to configure. Note that Google Wallet currently only supports shipping to the United States and United Kingdom.

This article shows how to configure your store for use with Google Wallet. There are several steps to this process as well as a few notifications regarding online shipping you will need to be aware of when implementing Google Wallet for your online store. Please read this article in its entirety before proceeding.

Getting Started

To integrate your store with Google Wallet:

1. First, you'll need to register for a Google Wallet account by going to http://wallet.google.com/sell.
2. Once you create an account, log in to Google Wallet and retrieve your *Merchant ID* and *Merchant Key* under the *Account Information* link.
3. In your store's *Admin Area*, go to *Settings* > *Payment* > *More Payment Types* and select the *Google Wallet* option.
4. Enter your *Merchant ID* and *Merchant Key* and click *Save*. SHOW

Configure Google Wallet to Communicate With Your Store

1. Log in to Google Wallet and click on the *Settings* tab. SHOW

In most other e-commerce environments this would have been a big job with plenty of technical complexity. You might have ended up hiring someone else to do it, you would probably have paid extra for the Google Wallet 'Module' and if you did it wrong and upset the Google gods you would probably be banned from taking Google payments without warning. There are so many other situations like this were Volusion makes it easy.

The other links under My resources simply take you to more specific parts of the knowledge base. If you have a spare half an hour download the latest manual by clicking on ***Manuals.*** More likely if you have a spare 5 minutes or are having a working tea break, click on ***Videos*** and take a quick video tour of some aspect of Volusion you haven't explored yet.

And absolutely make sure you check the ***Community*** link and the vast social site that Volusion have provided. 'Tips from the trenches' is full of money making tips and tricks.

My Support

Now some problems, usually the ones specific to your business, won't be in the knowledge base. For that you have the ticket system. You post a question (ticket), a Volusion expert sends you a reply. Lets try it out.

Click on ***Create ticket***.

Create ticket screen

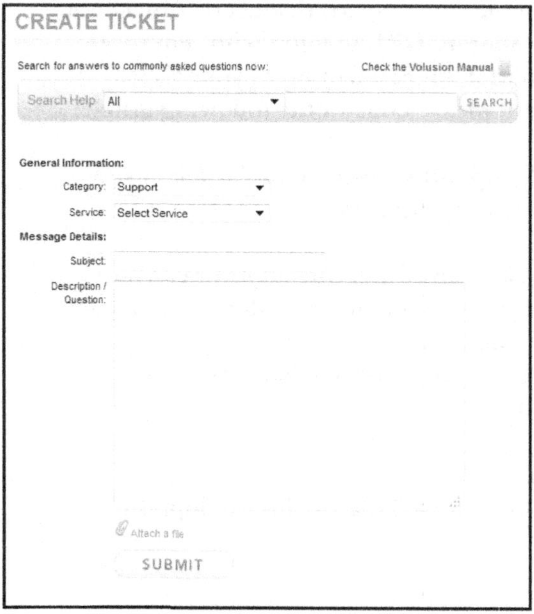

Enter your question, subject service and category. Press submit. My question was "What URL do I use when connecting to my store FTP" and I submitted at 14:33.

It took just over an hour for a reply.

"Hello,

Thank you for contacting Volusion. For

www.pixelprotector.com you can use the domain name or mjzkn.tfvkk.servertrust.com, the temporary URL to login with. For more information on connecting to your FTP account, please consult the following article:

http://support.volusion.com/article/using-your-volusion-ftp-account

If you have any other questions or concerns with this or any other issue, don't hesitate to contact us again.
Thanks for choosing Volusion and have a great day!

Jon M.
Here for you 24x7x365 Volusion Support ".

Which is exactly correct. Thanks Jon M!.

Actually I already new that but I just wanted to see how quick they were today.

My Account

Keep credit cards, billing history etc up to date.

My Store

This lets you look at all your store(s) (more in chapter 9 ;-)), select which store control panel to jump to. So MyVolusion really is the hub of your e-commerce and business world

Like so much in MyVolusion some of the options under My Store are self explanatory. But 2 links in particular deserve to be looked at in more detail. My Stats I will go into in chapter 9 but lets have a look at Manage FTP now.

My FTP

FTP is the system you use to manage all the files, folders and images stored on the actual web server where your store is hosted. In the main you don't need to worry about this unless you are designing your own store or hiring a non-Volusion specialist. But I just want to show you a quick and easy way to keep your store looking fresh.

You know those really cool rotating banners you see on the top of some of the nice examples I showed you back in the branding section? Well its a good thing to swap them around from time to time. Perhaps an offer has changed, there is something new you want to highlight or simply to freshen up your store for regular visitors.

Click on ***Manage FTP*** or just follow along if you don't have a Volusion account.

You see a drop down asking you to select which stores FTP you want to access.

select site for FTP

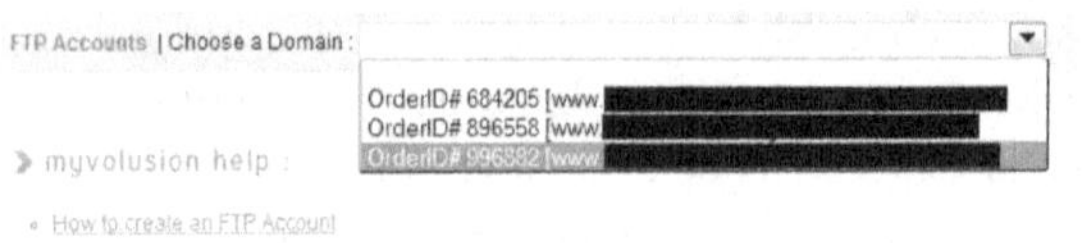

Click the site you want and proceed. If you are wondering why I keep referring to your sites, plural you will need to wait until chapter 9.

If this is your first login to FTP you will need to add an FTP account by clicking the ***Add*** button. Change the username and password to something discrete but memorable to you and accept the other settings by clicking ***Save***.

Now we need some free software. Grab a copy of FileZilla Client software from filezilla-project.org. Download it, double click to install and then run it. You will see something like this.

FileZilla

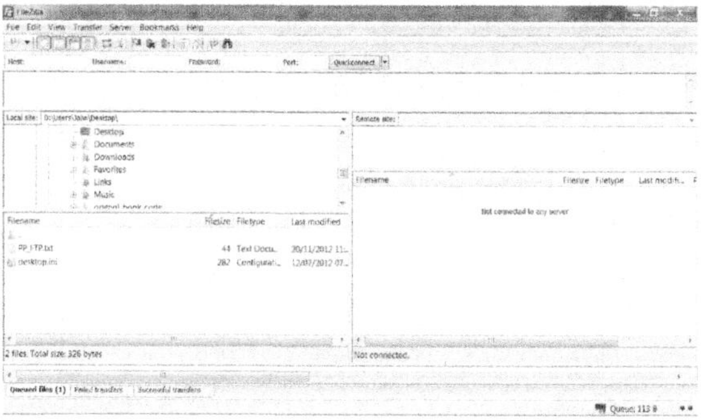

Here's how to change the banners we installed for you. If we didn't this is a good guide for how to change your files around in general. Have your new banners handy in a folder on your desktop.

First login by entering your stores web address, your FTP login and password in the places shown below. In the empty box called 'Port' type ***21***. Now press ***Quick Connect***.

On the right hand side you should have a part of the FileZilla window that looks like this.

FileZilla folders window

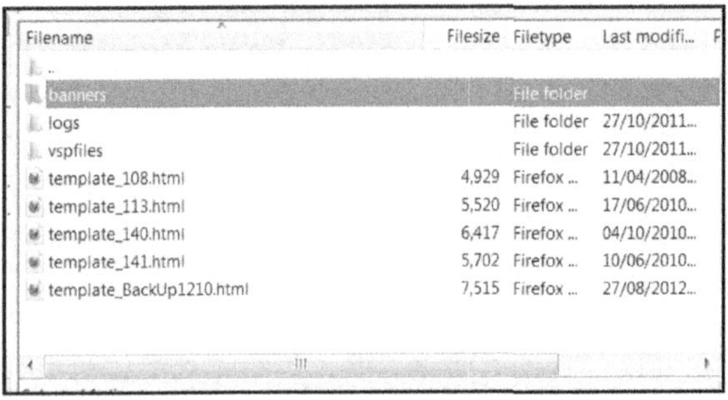

Double click the **banners** folder.

FileZilla - Inside the banners folder

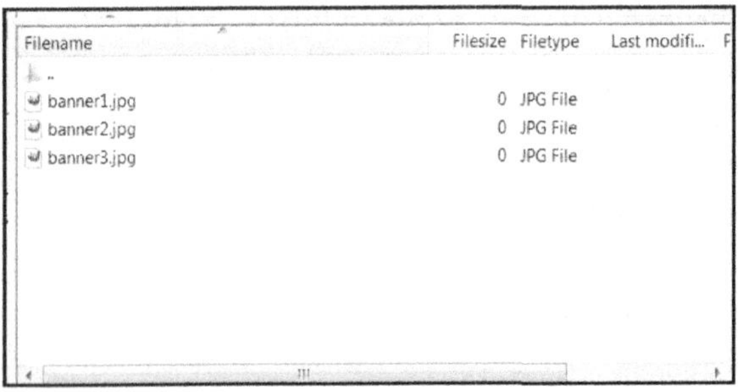

Now ***right click*** on the banner you want to replace. Rename it to something that makes it clear what it is and what it was. So **banner1.jpg** could become **old_banner1.jpg**.

Now select the new banner on your desktop. Drag it into an empty space in the banners folder in FileZilla.

Make sure you have named it the same name as the old banner by right clicking the new banner, selecting ***rename*** and calling it **banner1.jpg** (or whatever) if necessary. That's it. New banner installed.

My Domain

Everything you need to manage your portfolio of domain names, Cancel add, renew etc.

My Services

A quick click to Volusion services including, design, marketing and SEO.

MyVolusion reprise

Get to know MyVolusion like your own home because you can do just about everything from here.

Your ready now. Lets go and tell the world about your new store.

7

Volusion Marketing

By this stage you have a stunningly presented Volusion store that is optimized for the search engines. This chapter we are going to look into more ways to help and support your customers. But at the same time we want to bring in new customers and help our existing customers to consider more purchases.

First lets market with great content.

Writing articles

Visitors rarely want to read the whole article. They are usually looking for a fact or very specific piece of information. Try and make easy for them to find at the same time as compelling enough to keep reading.

Focus on readability

Focus on readability. If you have a subject people are interested in, you know about it, and you focus your efforts in making your pages easy to get information from, then people will like your articles. And if we work on the assumption that search engines know what people want, they will also rank you higher and more sites will want to link to you. So you win with humans and search engines.

Consider carefully who your website and the specific page you are working on are aimed at. Under what circumstances would somebody want to read your page? Is the page worded and structured in such a way as to accommodate their circumstances?

Do the most important pieces of information jump out of the page by being part of a short paragraph, table, bold or underline?

How smart are your customers?

Think about the level of expertise your customers have. What language or level of industry jargon will they like and what will bore them? Don't use technical jargon or clever words unless you are certain that is what your reader likes.

Don't use long words where short ones will do. Forget about preamble! Your first heading and paragraph should be 100 percent specific and lay out clearly what the rest of the article is about.

Definitely use colorful, interesting language but not at the expense of immediate clarity. The first heading should sum up the article: for example, you would put "How to write articles" and not "Hints and tips when getting started with writing".

Sell subtly

Don't 'flog' a product. It is perfectly acceptable to turn a word or phrase in your article into a link to a product, as long as it doesn't trick the reader into viewing the product.

Don't use too many product links. Links to information the reader is looking for are most important, or readers might find your site too hard to navigate and leave.

Don't forget the article is surrounded by your Volusion store template—products, specials, and so on. They will easily find your products when they are ready.

Don't promote your products unless it is appropriate. In every industry, there are products that are right for different people in different situations. If you are 100 percent honest when a product might not be suitable, your reader will subconsciously recognize your honesty.

If you recommend a cheap, reliable product that is appropriate in one situation, when the reader needs something top of the range, they are more likely to believe your writing.

'Speak proper like'

Grammar and spelling are very important. Spelling mistakes lose you credibility.

Grammar is something I have always struggled with. I have never been taught how to write well-structured content for any medium. But that is no excuse not to make it as good as you possibly can. I read and reread all my work to make it the best it can be. Then get a friend or colleague to check it.

What Now?

All good articles tell the reader what to do next. Perhaps to click a link to more information, sign up for your newsletter or look at a product. If your content has been written well, proved useful, and not been too pushy, you will have built trust even more trust for your brand.

SEO in articles

Headers, underline, italics, image filenames, article titles, and so on—that's called formatting is. It's all the different ways you can present information or add relevancy and appropriateness to the article.

Name your pictures and pages with relevant keywords and phrases. For example:

Nike-Bekam-Trainers-in-Red.jpg

not

img0786.jpg

Focus your effort on what is good for humans. Create an H2 heading containing the keywords/phrase at the start of the article. Use same keywords/phrases in the first paragraph. Consider making them bold or italic.

Use H3 and H4 headings generously and appropriately again with similar or identical keywords/phrases later in the article. Lots of well–ordered, clear, nested headings make your articles easily scan-able and more likely to be read in full.

Use links (with keywords/phrases) to relevant parts of the same page or other pages in your shop. All the above techniques not only make your article easier to scan, but they also highlight the key bits of information, making your article genuinely useful. When you make useful articles, visitors will like you, and people buy from people they like.

Keyword density

This is probably one of the most widely sought after pieces of information to do with SEO.

What percentage keyword density is perfect? That is, if your page has a hundred words how many of them should be the words you think people searching for you will use?

In a nutshell—sorry, I don't know. If you take Google for example, their formula for calculating page rank is a very closely guarded secret.

If somebody tells you the percentage is "x", don't hire them. The truth is that there probably is no specific percentage anyway.

It is in fact based on a publicly unknown and extremely complicated list of variables likely to include links to your site, their content, the rank of the site, and the page they appear on, the density, spacing, format, and the location on the page as well as the location of the page on your site and many more factors.

So how on earth do you optimize for such complexity? The most important thing you can do is make sure you choose the words your customers are likely to use. The ones you have already researched.

Use them in different formats and locations: headings, links, underlines, bold, and so on. Some should be near the end of the page, some in the links outside the main body of the page, and some in the pages linking to the page.

However, do not put more keywords or phrases than is natural to a human reader. If it sounds natural, looks natural, and uses the words you are targeting, that's good.

Quick tips

- If you have a complicated subject where you need to go into detail, this is not a problem. Try to keep the start of the article simple and build the complexity later in the article and pay extra attention to all the rest of the tips.
- Think and plan the structure of your article before you start writing. This includes deciding upon highly relevant, to-the-point titles and subtitles.
- Good and frequent subtitles divide up your article and help readers target what they want, and this makes the whole article easier to read.
- Use shorter paragraphs and sentences. They make your article easier to read.
- Use bulleted lists of key information. A bit like this one.
- Don't make the pages too long. Consider breaking the article into multiple articles if it seems heavy going to read it all.
- Most readers will scan the first line of a few titles and paragraphs to discover if

your article has what they want. Make the first sentence of each paragraph highly relevant and precise.

Don't panic

All this might seem a bit daunting, but try to write with all that guidance in mind. Always go through and edit your articles with the guidance in mind, but don't wait until it is perfect.

You wouldn't be reading this now if I had aimed for perfection.

Ask yourself: Is it useful? Is it clear and simple to scan and read? Is it professional-ish? If so, publish it. You can always revise it another time or react to feedback.

As I mentioned in Chapter 5, Codeaxa has writers who can thoroughly research and write articles about your industry for your store. So if you are thinking of outsourcing your writing then check out our packages on www.codeaxa.com.

Volusion content management

Here is how to publish your articles in your web store. Click on ***Design*** then ***Content***. Now click ***add***. You will see something similar to the picture over the page.

Volusion add content page

Enter the title, the article itself and don't forget all those meta-tags as discussed previously to be entered in the 'advanced' drop down below.

In the top right choose the page and location for your article and click ***save***.

Blogging

Remember you don't have to only write for your own web site. If you have written or received an article you are particularly proud of consider submitting it to industry blogs, news sites or if relevant issuing it as a press release. All of course can contain an inbound link to the appropriate part of your Volusion web store. And why not start your own blog and create a whole series of articles and news stories relevant to the industry you are in. Just remember not to simply re-post identical articles to what you already have on your Volusion site. This will definitely harm business in the medium term.

Newsletters/email marketing

Now that you have a growing collection of great articles why not share them with your customers. Only use articles you feel they would be genuinely interested in. For example a clothing customer might be interested in a sneak peek at the new range of something they previously purchased but less so in an industry centric article about the drought in India pushing up the price of cotton.

First thing we need to do is create some categories of newsletter so that customers can choose which if any they would like to receive. So in the clothing store you could create categories like 'coming soon' 'industry news' 'just shoes' and many more if necessary to suit your store requirements.

When customers create or login to their account they will have the option to subscribe or unsubscribe from these categories and when you write newsletters you will be able to assign them to categories to avoid any of your customers feeling like they are getting spam.

Creating newsletter categories

In Volusion select ***Marketing*** then ***News letters*** and press the ***Add*** button. Now scroll to the bottom of the page and click the ***edit*** button I am pointing to in the next image.

Editing newsletter categories

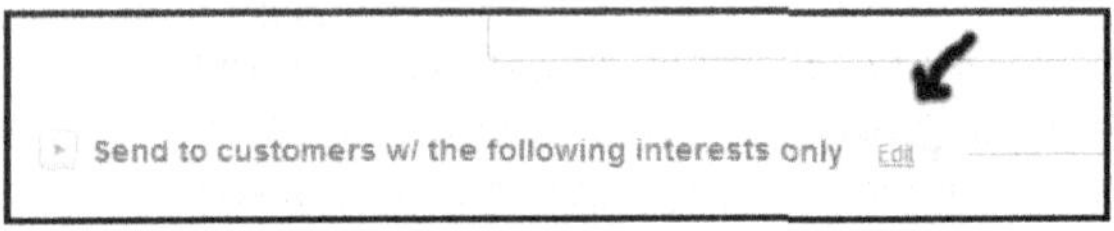

You will now be able to edit the default categories to make their names meaningful and relevant to your customers. Just click on the link of Newsletter 1 and change it. Then do the same for as many newsletters as you need.

Now go back to the add newsletter page. The quickest way is probably to select ***Marketing*** then ***News letters*** and press the ***Add*** button.

Fill out the required fields, they are all self explanatory or click on the little green question marks for the Volusion explanation. The two most important things is to schedule a date to send it in the date box on the right and select which categories of subscribers it should be sent to in the drop down at the bottom of the page. That's it.

A few guide lines. Make sure the product links are genuinely relevant and not overwhelming. Think carefully about the frequency that you send them. Unless your business is rapidly moving and your customers really want to know what is going on then once per month per category is probably enough.

Volusion marketing tools

This will be a whirlwind tour of some great Volusion marketing features not to be missed out on.

Gift certificates

These are a completely hassle free way to encourage additional sales. Unless you have a really good reason not to here is how to allow your customers to buy gift certificates.

Click on ***Settings*** then choose ***Config Variables*** and make sure 'Enable Gift' Certificates and 'Enable Price Edit' are both selected.

You have just enabled gift certificates. Now to configure a customer value configurable certificate. (Allow customers to choose the value of certificate they buy.)

Click ***Inventory*** then select ***Products*** and finally ***GFT*** in the products list.

Set the price as 0.0.

Scroll down to 'Advanced Info' and select 'Allow price edit'.

You can now add the gift certificate to any category or create its own category.

Coupons and discounts

Worried that your newsletters might not be exciting enough? Made a mistake that disappointed a customer and you want to win them back? No problem. Why not send out a money off voucher, percentage discount or multi-buy offer.

It is a breeze with Volusion. All you do is create the coupon/voucher configured to the type and quantity of discount mentioned above, assign it a duration/number of purchases and send its code to anyone you like or include it in a newsletter.

Click on ***Marketing*** then ***Coupons/Discounts***, finally click ***Add*** to configure your discount. A little tip make the code meaningful and enticing. shoes_10_1day_only.

Loyalty program

This could be the big one. If you have a deep, wide or consumable range then customers love being rewarded for loyalty. It makes them feel they are getting something that someone who is just making their first purchase isn't getting.

Fortunately what could be a complicated in-depth topic with no end of configuration issues is made into a couple of clicks with the Volusion Loyalty reward system called MyRewards.

Click on ***Marketing*** then ***MyRewards*** and we will go through some of the options.

The MyRewards setup screen Points for Cash)

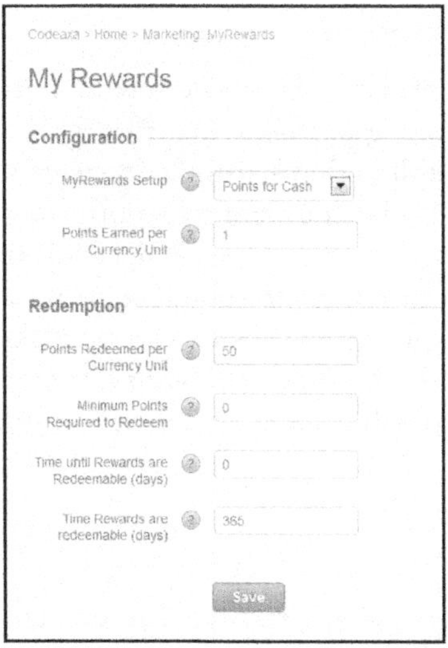

In the first drop down box you can choose to reward for cash amount spent or specific products purchased.

Choosing 'Points for products' is more long winded to configure but not complicated in any way. On the actual product page on the Advanced Info tab under 'Misc' you can choose how many, if any points that you want on a per product basis.

Here is how to configure Points for Cash.

Customer reviews

This is self explanatory but make sure they are enabled by clicking ***Settings*** then ***Config Variables***. Scroll to find 'Customer reviews' and enable them. And if you want to get off to a good start don't forget to loan some products to friends and family and ask them to submit some reviews. You can manage any reviews you get by clicking ***Customers*** then ***Customer Reviews***. So if you get any unreasonable ones you can choose not to show them.

Deal of the day

Just what the title suggests. Adds a prominent feature to your site highlighting to your customers what you think is the most special product today. Simply select ***Marketing*** then ***Deal of the day*** and fill out the form.

Using this regularly even if it is not every day keeps your site fresh and will catch the eye of shoppers who previously might not have been quite ready to buy and if deal of the day is implemented well in your custom template it can look brilliant too.

Video marketing

Have you got any promotional or manufacturer videos you want to add to your site? You can do this in two main ways.

The first is by visiting the video on YouTube and using the YouTube tools to create an embed link. You can then simply copy and paste this into the HTML of the article, product, category or even newsletter in the place of your choice.

The best way to add video to a product page however is to use the Volusion system as the videos will appear precisely as your template wants them too.

Select ***Inventory*** and then ***Products***. Click on the product you want to add video to. Scroll down and see the Volusion YouTube video management section. Expand it if necessary.

YouTube video management

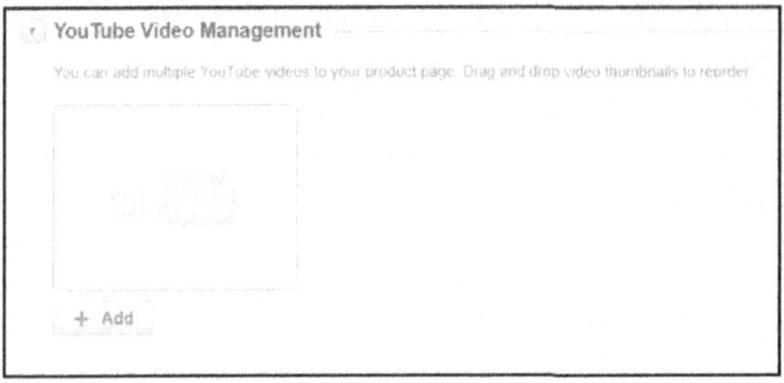

Just click ***add*** and paste the YouTube URL. That's it. The videos appear on your page formatted as the designer intended. You can add up to four videos and can drag their thumbnail images around to change their order of appearance.

Affiliates

Affiliation is were you recruit other people to advertise your products on their web site and then reward them when a sale is made because of a visit they sent you.

This type of tracking and management is complex to implement and there are many affiliate software solutions that cost hundreds of pounds and are extremely difficult to integrate. You know what I am going to say next? Volusion...

Here is how to do it. It really is impossible to over state how much complexity and potential expense this Volusion feature saves. Think about it. How do you know which affiliate sent a customer, whether a sale was made, how much they have earned, how to pay them. How do the affiliates keep track of their performance, know that the system is fair, implement the system on their site? There are so many complex issues and Volusion just makes it work like this.

- You know somebody who wants to be an affiliate.
- You make them a special affiliate account.
- They log in to their account and do all the work.
- You both get a report of how much has been earned/needs to be paid.

Here is each step in a bit more detail. Making an affiliate account comes first. Select ***Marketing*** then ***Affiliates*** and click on ***Add.***

Add affiliate page

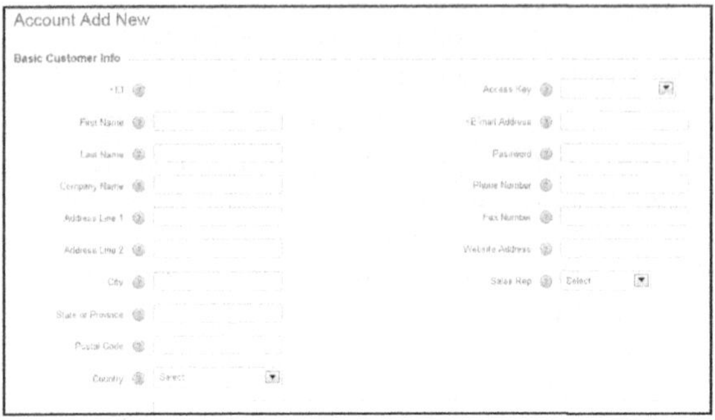

Simply add the obvious fields like name, address, telephone etc. Set ***Access Key*** to 'Partner Affiliate'. Email your new affiliate there login details.

When they login and click on ***Visit my affiliate page*** they can see how much they have earned, how many potential customers they sent.

Affiliate statistics

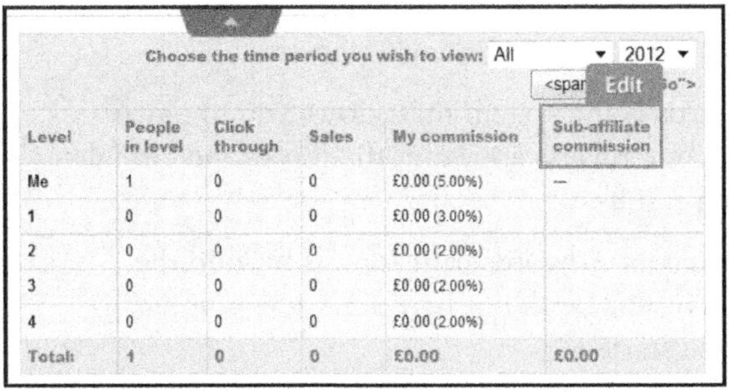

Choose the time period you wish to view: All 2012

<span Edit Go">

Level	People in level	Click through	Sales	My commission	Sub-affiliate commission
Me	1	0	0	£0.00 (5.00%)	—
1	0	0	0	£0.00 (3.00%)	
2	0	0	0	£0.00 (2.00%)	
3	0	0	0	£0.00 (2.00%)	
4	0	0	0	£0.00 (2.00%)	
Total:	1	0	0	£0.00	£0.00

And the URL they need to use on their web site so the Volusion system can track them.

Affiliate tracking URL

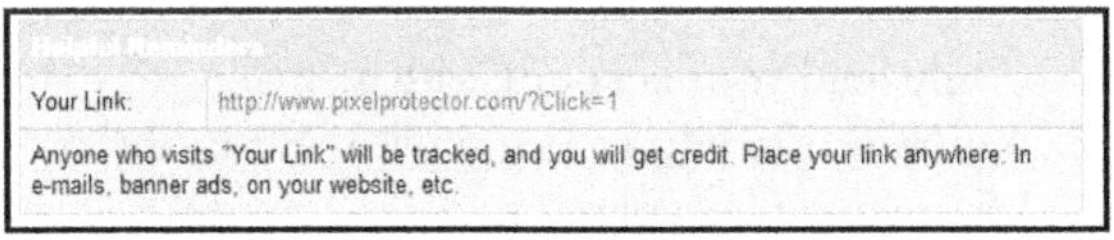

This stunning system is part of the Volusion Gold package for no extra cost.

Adwords

Adwords is not part of Volusion but it is such a potentially powerful tool it can't go without a mention. If you created an Adwords account back in Chapter 5 to use the keyword tools, you probably noticed that there is rather allot more to Adwords than just Keyword statistics.

Adwords is the system that allows you to pay to have your adverts appear at the top of the Google search results.

Running an Adwords campaign is beyond the scope of this book but here are a few pointers to get you started.

The Adwords interface is not difficult. You can easily create a campaign, create some adverts and then set the amount you are prepared to pay per click. Three tips to avoid financial ruin. Well not quite but to save wasting any money. Targeting and configuring an Adwords campaign takes time, refinement and a bit of skill too, so...

- Only load your account with a small amount of credit to begin with. No more than you are prepared to lose.
- Remember about the long tail keyword searches being more ready to buy?
- Read more on Adwords and/or consult with a professional SEO.

More marketing

Actually there are many more ways of marketing your Volusion store but they are so significant and powerful they deserve a chapter all to themselves.

Ever heard of Facebook and Twitter? Read on.

8

Social

You can't have been alive these past few years and failed to notice the social media revolution. Businesses have made billions, governments have fallen and presidents have been re-elected because of it.

The bad news is there is no silver bullet for social media success, the good news is that the skills needed are easily nurtured and the budgets required are not excessive.

In this chapter we will take a fast look around the two key social networks at the moment, FaceBook and Twitter.

FaceBook

FaceBook is massive. Sure there is loads of talk about problems with their share price, monetizing their audience and privacy. But guess what. FaceBook is still growing and shows no signs of slowing down. What this part of the book is for is to get you off on the right track to successfully building an audience and keeping it engaged.

Getting an audience

You need to create a 'page' and set about promoting it and making a cool place to visit.

One of your first decisions is to decide on your pages profile. Are you going to name it after your shop, yourself or something else entirely? There is no right or wrong answer here. You need to decide what it is about you, your industry or shop that is the most marketable/interesting.

If your shop is really interesting and dynamic, it creates its own news then the decision is easy. The page should be named after your store. If you are genuinely perceived as a cool dude(dudette) and you look the part as well, then name it after you. If not then you can create a profile that focuses on an interesting and dynamic aspect of your store or business that is marketable. Its a brand all over again but one that works best for maintaining an audience rather than simply a shop.

Once you know what your going to call your FaceBook page you then need to create excellent images. One for the header of your page and one for your profile image. If you have a really nice logo you can use this along with the text of your profile name.

If you are using your self as your page profile then obviously you need a really flattering head and shoulders portrait. If that isn't possible then a professionally made graphic interpretation of a photo will do. If that isn't possible then you might have made the wrong choice of profile picture.

How can I be so shallow? If your image does not fit the perceived persona of the audience you are trying to attract then use your logo instead. That's the world we live in. People will be making split second decisions whether to check out your page and it will largely depend on if they like the look of you.

The header banner should be all encompassing of your brand. Remember all the things that had to be in the design of your site? Well now you need to squeeze trust, mission, likeability, product range and more all into a banner. Oh and without breaking any of FaceBook's rules. No call to action, contact information or prices. If you annoy FaceBook they will ruin your dreams of social media success, permanently, without warning or chance of appeal.

Building an audience

When your page is created you need to create some content for your page. These should be a selection of different types of media. You can probably reuse some of the more topical media you already created for the shop. Your best guides from YouTube, latest product photos, great customer reviews (with the customers permission) etc.

Once you have a good foundation of interesting content its time to call on your close family and friends to 'like' your page and post witty comments on your posts.

Now you have a good foundation and you don't look like your 'Billy no-mates', lets try and start to build a genuine audience.

Sign into FaceBook and use the little drop down selector in the top right corner of the screen to use FaceBook as your page. This means that everything you do will show you as your page, not your personal profile.

Step 1: Visit appropriate pages and profiles. Like them and leave comments where you genuinely feel you want to or have something to say.

Step 2: Post more, topical interesting content to your page and engage/respond to what is being talked about on your page.

Step 3: Repeat from step one until you have one billion monthly active users.

OK, I admit I am being a bit nonchalant but I wanted to make a point. If you only take one thing away from this far-to-fast FaceBook guide it should be this. The only way to attract, engage, grow and keep an audience on FaceBook is to genuinely engage with them. Get to know the top posters on your page, participate, keep visiting and engaging with others in your industry and related areas of interest.

Just when it might be beginning to sound easy there is one enormous pitfall that I have sort of covered already but is worth making absolutely clear.

I mentioned about leaving comments were you 'genuinely' have something to say. If people/businesses think you are only there to get attention they will click a button to report you as spam. Enough people do this and you will get the same treatment from FaceBook that we talked about earlier with regard to breaking their rules.

Paid advertising

You might have heard about FaceBook's advertising problems. Not least of which is its inability to monetize mobile users which are becoming more numerous than desktop users. Paid advertising on FaceBook at the moment, in my opinion is only worth it in a very few niches or for the very biggest brands.

FaceBook goals

Certainly you want to get as many page likes as you can but don't become obsessed. It is better to have one properly engaged user than 10 who like the page and never come back.

The key to this is regular, but not too regular updates. Once a day for all but the most popular page is probably too much. A couple of times a week is easily enough. Make sure your posts are absolutely, genuinely interesting. The true mark of success in FaceBook marketing is not page likes but post positive comments and shares. When they do this there comments and the original post can appear on the news feeds of their friends. This is true viral marketing. People who comment on and share your posts are your true brand advocates.

So FaceBook marketing really is a way to boost your Volusion shop but it shouldn't be an obsession and shouldn't drain your wallet.

Volusion on FaceBook

Ever wanted your own store on FaceBook? So as you build your following and engage bigger audiences they can browse and purchase your products directly on FaceBook? Its a breeze with Volusion. Here is how to do it.

The first thing to do is to link your FaceBook account to your Volusion store. In your Volusion control panel click ***Marketing*** then ***Social.*** and finally press ***Sign in***, next to the FaceBook logo. Sign in to FaceBook and your done. You can do the same for Twitter while your here. More soon on Twitter.

Preparing your FaceBook store

Select Marketing then ***FaceBook store***. If you were expecting a challenge at this point you will be pleasantly surprised. The way it works is that by selecting your options on this page you will configure what is known as a feed. That is all the information necessary to sell on FaceBook. Then as the final step you will go to FaceBook and install the Volusion FaceBook app on your page. This app reads and displays the feed. Done.

Here are the key options to configure to create your FaceBook feed.

Enable the feed:

Select your top 10 to 20 products. Any more might make your page confusing.

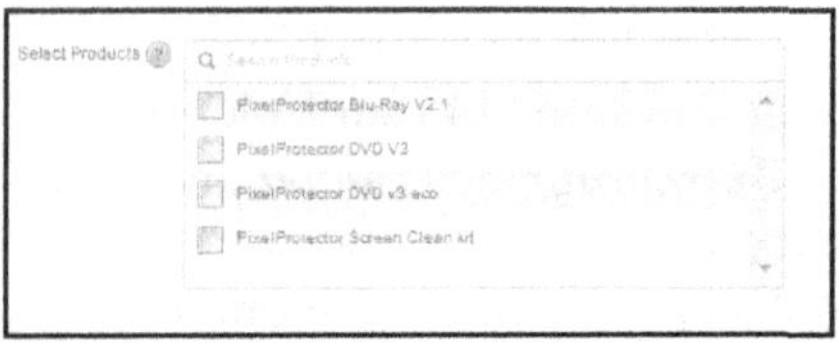

Configure product sorting and deal of the day settings.

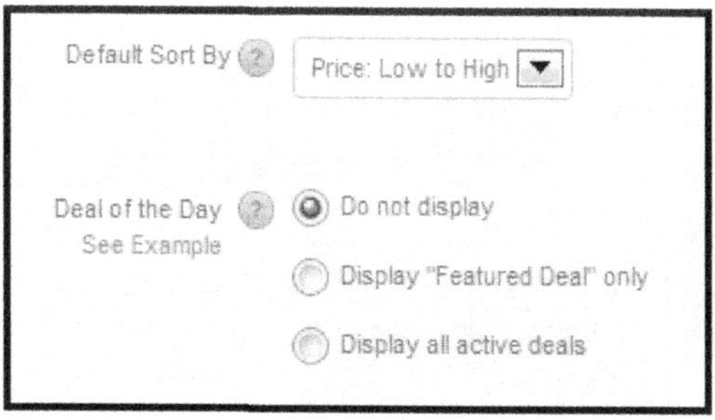

Optionally include a discount for liking your page. A good idea if you can. People like discounts and we like likes!

Configure discounts

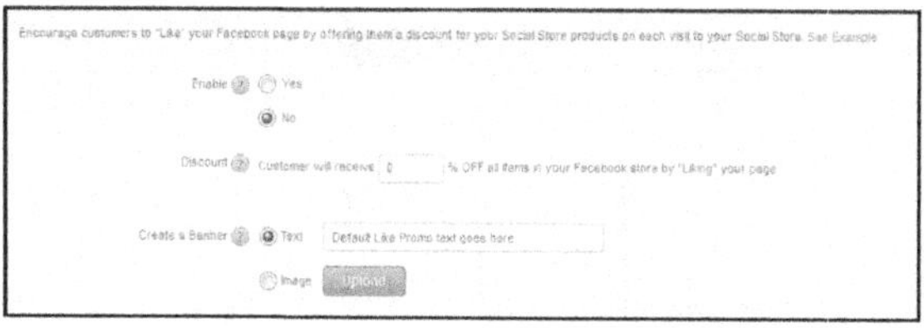

Design your store.

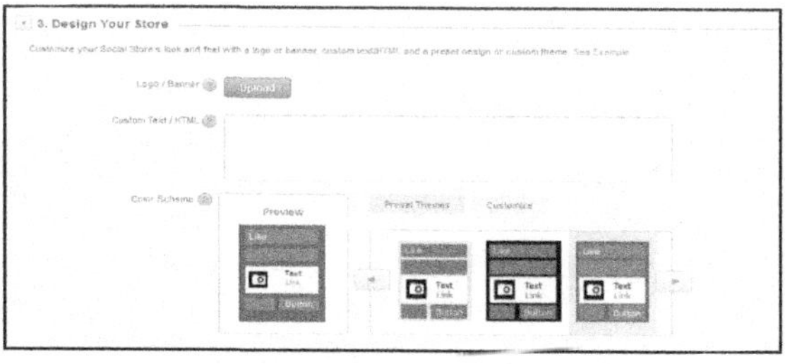

Sample store to help get a feel for what does what.

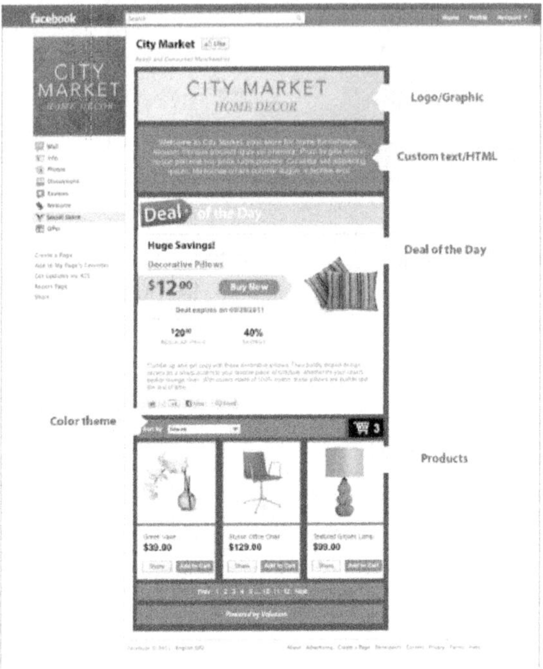

Finally click the button below and follow the simple instructions to install the Volusion app to your page.

Save your configurations.

Designing your FaceBook store is very much simpler than your Volusion store but if you can't make it match your brand 100% then please seek help.

Twitter

This guide assumes you already have a Twitter account. Link your Volusion control panel to your Twitter account, if you haven't already, by clicking ***Marketing*** then ***Social***, and finally, ***Sign In***, on the Twitter logo.

Projecting your brand

This comes back to part of the paragraph of prosperity about being liked and trusted. Login to your Twitter account. Click on the settings cog icon in the top right and you should see, on the left, the option to click on Design. Do so and you will see the image over the page.

Twitter design screen

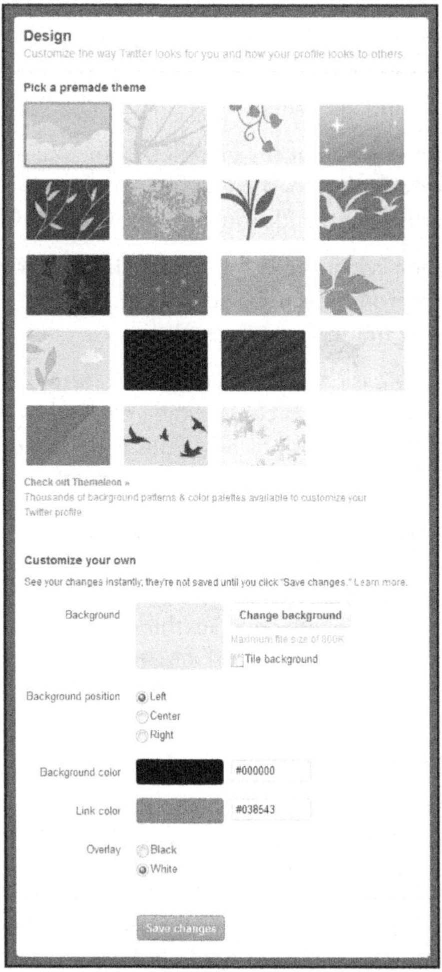

The first thing to say about this screen should be obvious by now. The first option to pick a pre-made theme isn't the one for you. You want to project your unique brand from your shop consistently and accurately.

You can reuse some of the graphics from your store. For example a logo could be used for your profile picture or an endearing image of yourself.

You can then select the colors to match your store for the background or use a suitable image that projects your brand.

This could be easier said than done as a store template doesn't always contain the graphical assets that fit a Twitter profile. If this is the case for you there are two options.

Keep it really simple. A completely plain background in one relevant color or a professionally designed profile. A good design company will not charge you anything like as much as they did for the initial design to convert a few assets and position them on Twitter for you.

Following others

This is really easy. Search on Twitter for the keywords and phrases related to your business.

Check out the profiles that come up in the results and look for people and brands that look like they know what they are talking about and have professional looking profile page as well. Follow them. You might learn something and there is a very good chance they and some of their followers will follow you back.

Building a following

If nobody is following you nobody is listening. You could also argue that even if you are being followed many of them are still not listening! The importance of a quality, relevant following cannot be overstressed.

Getting quality, relevant followers is not as hard as you might think.

The best way to build a following is to tweet. And make sure your tweets are genuinely interesting, topical and varied. This way you will get followers interested in many aspects of your business or industry.

If your tweets are really good, eventually some of your followers might reply to one of your tweets. This means that not only does a direct link (@yourusername) appears on their time-line next to their reply but the reply along with the link is broadcast to all their followers as well! And in turn might decide to reply or follow you.

Here is the unfortunate thing. If your tweets are not interesting and relevant to your followers they will stop following you. So we need to compose great tweets.

How often to tweet

What tweeting frequency is right for you will depend upon how frequently things change and how dynamic your industry is. Test out different frequencies and look at what popular people in your industry are doing.

Composing your tweets

Every tweet should be meaningful on its own or add something to the conversation

Regular Tweets – Easy. Just answer the question. "What are you doing now".

"I am considering stocking the new Nike Bekams in size 12. Do grown men want them too?"

Never lose focus on making it relevant to your audience. Be consistent but not too frequent and keep it non commercial. (See Sales tweets).

Broadcasting – All your regular tweets should be relevant and personal, from you. The exception to this rule is when you just want to broadcast something really significant. "Fire at Nike bekams factory kills 3 ". They should not be the standard format of your tweeting. Impersonal all the time is un-interesting.

Humor – If you've got it flaunt it. Jokes are great and there is plenty on Twitter. A good joke can keep your followers keen. But if you haven't got it probably best to leave the jokes to someone else.

Questions – If you ask for an opinion you can get responses without being socially indebted. Also, if you are lucky you might provoke a discussion, lots of replies and the publicity that goes with it.

Replying & Re-tweeting – Can't think of anything to say? No problem. Find somebody who can. Search for the phrases you are interested in and find something relevant to post a reply to.

This will tell all your followers what you are looking at. And who knows, the other persons tweet might inspire something original from you. And if your really stuck just re-tweet (copy) someone's message. They will probably be pleased you did.

Sales tweets – The simplest most subtle way of promoting your site is to add a link to your homepage with occasional tweets. The tweet does not have to suggest a purchase or promote a product it simply says what you want to say and links to your homepage so people can click and see what you are all about.

More direct but still fairly subtle is to ask peoples opinion on a very specific aspect of a product or service. Ask for feed-back on the product itself, the way you have described or photographed it. You can do this easily through the Volusion control panel. Just type your Tweet and then select the product or category below and Volusion will do the rest.

This could generate some useful feedback and even some orders.

Tweeting summary

So basically you can tweet anything you like as long as it is in some way of value to your followers.

Try and develop a style and character that fits you and your business. Stick to a few minutes per day or even per week.

The next chapter

I have been bombarding you with information and I have to confess that the most crucial piece of information hasn't been given yet.

I am not holding back because I am mean or anything but simply because the real secret to success in any e-commerce business, which I reveal in the next chapter, requires the knowledge that we have acquired thus far.

It will all become plain very soon.

9

Your business in the future

How do you see your business in the future. Are you aiming for a small, trusted business that is perhaps considered an authority in its field? Do you want to be the next Amazon or are your goals somewhere in the middle? Whatever your business goals I believe it is important to consider why we are doing this at all.

Why?

I have been alluding to the 'why' all the way through the book. I thought it worth actually coming out and saying it though so it is clear. So why are we doing this?

Is it because we want the prestige of a successful business? Perhaps. Is it because we know that running our own e-commerce store is much more likely to make us wealthy than running someone else's? It could just be for the thrill of it. Whatever answer or answers the 'why are we doing this' question throws up for you, one of those answers will likely have to do with money.

That's fine but lets refine things further. Why do we want that money? And now we are getting nearer the real answer. At this point we will be coming out with answers like security, providing for our families and perhaps other noble goals like giving to charity etc.

But why would we do even these things? Simple. Happiness and contentment of the people we choose and the security of that happiness and contentment.

How happiness and contentment is arrived at for any given individual will vary of course but lets just keep in mind why we are here and then we can make sure that everything we do advances us towards those goals rather than move us farther away.

How?

Does long hours and stress, in itself provide you with your goals. Of course not, although we probably accept that a certain amount of both those things will be required along the way to achieving them. So if we accept that setting up an e-commerce store, even a Volusion store involves incredibly hard work and probably a little bit of stress, can we just relax and let the money roll in once it is up and running?

Not quite but here is a few ideas for you to think about.

Perpetualism

We need to create a system that provides our goals. Now how much you need to earn to do this will vary depending upon your specific goals but the one thing that remains constant for all of us is the security part. '..security of that happiness and contentment.'

We need ongoing consistency of income. The way to achieve this in e-commerce is as follows.

Measure, optimize and improve

And here is how we do it. First of all we measure. There are a number of tools available to us.

Volusion stats

There are an abundance of reports you can generate in Volusion and here is how to get them.

In your control panel click on ***Reports*** then ***Reporting***, followed by pressing the ***Create/edit report*** button.

Create/edit report screen

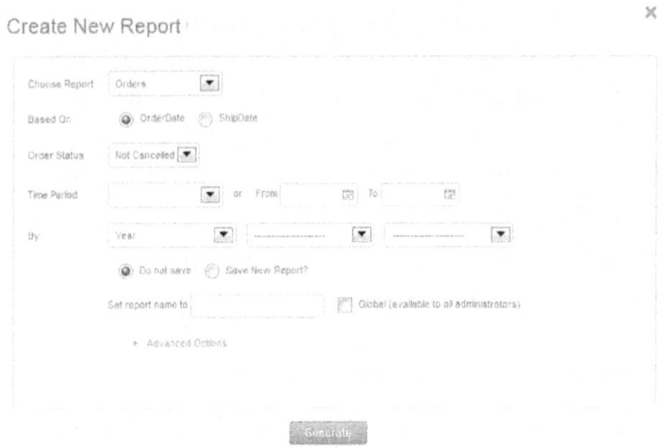

The first thing to look at here is the Choose report drop down. There are six different report types and each can by custom configured to your requirements. Amongst the most useful are the product and category views. These reports let you know just how popular- to look at- not necessarily buy any given product is. You can then compare this with say a sales report for the same period.

Are you getting hundreds of page views but no sales? Time to reinvent how the product is presented, described or priced. Good percentage of sales on a high margin product but not many views? Time to advertise this page with Google Adwords and improve SEO as well.

Exactly the same measurements can be used for the category pages as well.

Cart abandonment

Click on Abandoned/Live carts. You will probably see a fairly meaningless, hopefully quite short list of carts where the customer didn't complete the sale.

Abandoned cart report

So what can we actually glean from this? First of all the volume of cart abandonment's could be an indication of category structure, product/category description or available payment methods(have you got all the options people want). Here is the silver bullet.

Scan down the list and notice that occasionally people sign up for a store account *before* they abandon their cart. You can see the blanked out details of one such person in the image. Contacting this person could be the best phone call you ever made. Ring them and ask them if they want a free voucher in return for discussing their experience and reasons for non-purchase. If you get loads of abandonment's you could compose a standard email and send it to them all. Perhaps include a small discount voucher. Not so much to get the sale, although that would be nice, but to get the information you need to avoid future cart abandons.

Adwords

Look at how your Adwords is performing. Create multiple versions of the same advert and rotate when they are shown Different words and phrases might seem arbitrary to us but never forget that we are searching for the prospective buyer who is as near to the purchasing decision as possible. Differently worded adverts will produce surprisingly different results. And here is the news. It is rarely, if ever possible to predict which adverts will work. Add to that the adverts that work, sometimes, will change over time.

If a keyword/phrase brings buyers but not enough to make it worthwhile then look at reducing the price you pay to see if it still brings in any buyers. And conversely if a word/phrase is stunningly successful is it profitable to increase it?

Concentrate higher bids on longer phrases because the people typing longer phrases are more likely to have their credit cards in their hand.

It is fine to have casual browsers read your articles and click in from regular search results but when you are paying for the visit you need to make sure it is profitable.

Analytics

Google Analytics is trivial to setup with Volusion and provides a wealth of data and statistics that can be used to measure, optimize and improve.

The diversity, depth and sheer volume of data that can be obtained from Adsense can be overwhelming but there is one really simple statistic that can be used to great effect.

Find your most popular pages and make them a priority for the optimization described in a minute with regard to products and articles.

...

So if we measure and optimize in the ways we discussed we will constantly be creating a better experience for our customer a higher return on investment for ourselves and a more prominent presence on the search engines.

Statistical analysis of web site data is a worthy subject for a whole book and it is well worth reading one. My company can also give you guidance/manage your Adwords/Analytics campaign for you at the same time as looking out for those potentially profitable data spikes that the

Codeaxa experts are trained to spot. Drop us a line at www.codeaxa.com.

We can also optimize and improve by adding and expanding.

Articles

Remember all those articles we expertly crafted a few chapters back? Well its time to make them better. Open up your articles one at a time re-read them and think about the following.

How can I make them more up-to-date? Can I optimize them better for the search engines? Can I link to newer or more relevant parts/products of my store? Can I improve the grammar? Using all the concepts of writing for the Web, can I make the article more interesting?

Doing this does even more than it might first appear. By doing all of the above you don't just create a better, more optimized, interesting article. You also signal to the search engines, through their complicated algorithms and to your readers through their subconscious, that the article is more relevant and trustworthy. And guess what? The search engines send more people and the people like it and follow your advice/buy your products more.

Products

If you really know your industry then this might feel this bit is like teaching you to suck eggs. But updating your products is so much more than stocking the right stuff at the right time.

Look at all the advice above for refreshing your articles and apply that to all the different parts of your product description. As trends change are the products featured on your category home pages still the right ones. Is there a mega-trend going on in your industry at the moment that deserves featuring on your rotating homepage banner? Is the image the latest the manufacturer provides? Can you swap out some of the older images for new ones?

Yes, get the right stock. But present it in the right order and constantly improve and refresh the way they are presented and described.

Refreshing

You have probably read the section about FTP and refreshing your banners, we have just talked about refreshing images and articles but what about your site, template including branding and logo?

Brand refreshes can work miracles. Improve confidence, create a feeling of being new and build further on that critical perception of like and trust.

If your as old as me you will remember Proctor & Gamble. To most of my generation the name is almost synonymous with monopoly, corporate irresponsibility and killing fluffy bunnies.

Look at them now with their warm, loveable baby protecting P&G image and you can see the power of a brand refresh!

You can do partial refreshes and major refreshes. Check out my sample e-commerce to-do list for more ideas.

Putting it all together

Now just incase this is getting a bit intricate or muddled I will lay it out for you in precise terms.

Day, week, month, year in the life of a successful e-commerce entrepreneur.

Having said so much about what to do, when to do it might be helpful too. I would suggest the plan below would probably suit a growing e-commerce business with perhaps 100 *core* (at least 1 sold every few days) products over 10 categories and perhaps 10 to 50 *core* articles.

Daily e-commerce to-do list (Monday - Friday)

Job description	***(Minutes)***
Improve 2 articles.	30
Assess statistics and make changes.	30
Enhance 2 products.	30
Tweak 1 category home page.	5
Tweak the home page	1
Twitter/Facebook	10

Weekly e-commerce to-do list (Saturday morning)

Job description	***(Minutes)***
Write 1 new article.	180
Overhaul 1 category page	60
Overhaul the homepage	30

Yearly e-commerce to-do list

Job description	***(Time)***
Major template refresh	1 week
Minor brand enhancement	1 day
Major range refresh/assessment	1 week
Implement big secret?	2-6weeks

If you have a product which is especially key or an article which needs updating more frequently then obviously do so. The above is just a guide and to facilitate further discussion.

So the security of our success lies in the perpetualism or ongoing, repeating and consistent nature of our actions to measure, optimize and improve our business. Perpetualism isn't in most dictionaries but it best describes what we are aiming for.

Now what about if there was one more magic element we could add into our perpetual system that would seriously propel us towards our goals? Perhaps even prompt us to rewrite them with bigger ones.

The big secret to e-commerce success

The big secret isn't really a secret. It is more the specific manner of application of already proven conventional business practices along with one of the aspects of e-commerce income that produces a little known and highly desirable outcome. First the aspect of e-commerce income I am referring to is its passive nature.

Passive income

You have, at this stage, an opportunity for a little bit more than just paying the bills. I am not suggesting that we should, all or any of us, try and be extremely wealthy entrepreneurs.

There isn't anything wrong with that though. I am not suggesting we should, all or any of us, be big business people and dominate our markets, although that is OK as well.

I am not even suggesting that we should consider e-commerce, Volusion, or any other e-business tool to be anything more important than just that, a mere tool. But it would be negligent of me, having strung you along for more than a 150 pages, not to double check if you fully realized the power and potential of what you just started.

I admire people who work hard. And to have a successful e-commerce business, you have to work very hard indeed. But (and its a big but), unlike a high-powered job or conventional self-employment, a self-built e-commerce store offers the opportunity for income without the massive time constraints and life-dominating commitment required by most other businesses and by every form of employment.

I am not trying to describe an income that is necessarily big, although it can be, but an income that you control and not one that controls you.

Starting a business like this should not be the precursor to a full-time job, working for yourself. In fact, just the opposite can be true.

What I am trying to get to is this: **Volusion, when used efficiently, can be the start of a significant passive income. That is, an income**

that keeps coming in, even when you are not actually working on it.

Duplicate & diversify

So as well as managing yourself out of your time commitments we need to look at securing and increasing the income. Increases are found not just through improving your current store but by duplicating it. Security of income is found by diversifying all your streams of revenue.

Want proof? Go to Dixons.co.uk. Search for something specific. Then do the exact same thing on pcworld.co.uk and currys.co.uk. They aren't just owned by the same parent company, they run off the exact same database and central warehousing system. Even the product descriptions are identical. And they have been doing this for many years, long before the PC World/Curry's bricks and mortar merger. There are so many more examples as well. Electrical retailers who use the exact same catalog but different presentation for a wholesalers web site. Broad range sites which also have multiple niche sites run off of the same stock, probably operated by the same set of staff in a single office.

Exactly how you decide to duplicate and diversify, is of course dependent on your strategy and your business. But just be sure to take away the fact that your next e-commerce venture will take a fraction of the time that the original one did and each and every diversification and duplication will increase the "security of happiness and fulfillment", that we talked about previously.

Why not have a chat with me about duplicating and diversifying your business. Or grab a copy of my book, "Wealth Creation Online " from Amazon.

Nicks top ten rules for success

So we have looked at an awful lot of specifics as well as a few general points to make sure that our Volusion business is the best it can possibly be. What follows are some guiding principles which we can use to make sure we stay on the right path but without worrying about the details. I don't claim ownership of these principles or the way in which the are worded but I am responsible for choosing whether to live by them and if I am not, that something other than a vacuum replaces them.

Rule 1 - Get out of your comfort zone

I honestly don't believe that much good will come to anybody if they remain in their comfort zone. Businesses grow, wealth is created and ideas formed when working outside of where you feel at ease.

Remember that ancient human instinct that we discussed in Chapter 2? Well you can make it work for you. Put yourself in an uncomfortable position and your mind will work harder to achieve success.

This doesn't mean you should go out on a limb and risk all your capital. Make sure the uncomfortable position is pre-planned and you have pre-determined next steps to advance along a well thought out plan. You might amaze yourself. Comfort is an illusive trick to make sure you never do anything too great.

Rule 2 - Stand up for yourself and your business

In this country we have a much overlooked gift of law and order. If you find that a competitor or even a colleague is holding you back through intimidation move on any way. Our ancient brain perceives threats which don't exist anymore. If somebody physically intimidates you, walk up to them smile, shake their hand and then go and get on building your business regardless of what they may think, how big they are or whatever else the ancient part of your brain tries to use against you.

Rule 3 - Practice solving your own problems

I don't mean the small stuff. If you don't know what button to press in Volusion then ring them up, don't waste time hunting around. But the really big stuff, the fundamentals. Which product, which design, how much to borrow. It will train your business brain to function instinctively like your ancient survival brain. In time, you will have a killer edge over your competitors.

Rule 4 - Do it anyway

Whatever is worrying you in life, be sure to accept the worst thing that could possibly happen, always quantify what the worst outcome could be in any given situation. Then get on with it anyway.

It is very unlikely that the worst thing that could happen to you will be anywhere near as bad as the cloud of undefined consequences that will hang over you if you don't do it. When we have nothing to worry about we are not doing much, and not doing much may supply us with plenty of future worries.

Make a plan, understand the risks, mitigate for them and get on with it.

Rule 5: Don't expect life to be fair

Life is not fair! never has been, never will be. You make your own luck in this world. Remove the words " not fair" from your vocabulary and you will be in a better place.

Rule 6 - Keep moving forward

Never stop challenging yourself in life. Never stop doing new things in your business and life. Make it a goal to be better then yesterday.

Japanese Kaizen concept says. "Small daily improvements will eventually result in huge advantages"

So basically keep repeating rule 1 and you won't go far wrong.

Rule 7 - Always be courageous in your dealings

Remember that courage is not the absence of fear but rather knowing what to do in the presence of fear....Be courageous! as fortune will favor the brave.

Rule 8 - Plan and measure everything of importance

We have talked about this already but here is a couple of cool quotes that I like.

Plan out your day your week your month your year then you will have a plan for life. Any thing that is measured will improve.

Planning without action is futile, action without planning is fatal.

Rule 9 - Never quit

Never give up on your dreams! When you get to the point of wanting to quit, DON'T, you are probably closer than ever to achieving your goal.

Rule 10 - Keep your sense of humor alive and always find a reason to smile.

Have a bounce in your step, lighten up! No one is in control as much as they would like to think they are.

Bare in mind that we are not here for long, we should at least make sure we enjoy our time here!

If you don't have a sense of humor then it might be worth getting one. You don't need to be funny just be able to see the funny side of hard times.

"People of humor are always in some degree people of genius".

It can't be that easy?

Some of you might have read books that promise wealth, success or happiness if you will just follow some fluffy rules in your life. And, of course some of my ten rules were a bit fluffy too. The trick is to combine the big fluffy rules with the smaller details.

If you have a store, and you should at least be well on your way, that conforms to the paragraph of prosperity then all you need to do is fix your goals firmly in your mind or perhaps in a picture frame on your wall and get on, doggedly applying the details.

The problem with technical books is they lack the fluffy bits and the problem with the fluffy books is they tend to be written by people who's only qualification is that they have made themselves successful teaching people the fluffy bits. This doesn't easily translate into success for the reader.

No it won't be easy but you know exactly what you can achieve with a Volusion store and now you also know how to achieve it. Set it up right and then perpetually improve, refine, diversify and expand' keeping in mind what you have learned from your results and experience.

So knowing how to shift your e-commerce business towards a virtually passive income at the same time as using the duplication and diversification techniques that work so well with our e-commerce model. Your future really can be anything you want it to be. Not, as I have said, just wealthy but so much more as well.

Picture this...

It's 6 o'clock on Monday morning. You are not really looking forward to another gruelling week at the office.

And then you remember you don't do that anymore. You started your own online business, made it successful then duplicated and diversified it.

You pour a coffee. It smells good. You sit in your favourite chair and switch on your tablet. You check your e-mails.

You see you have made some sales overnight. You log into your Volusion control panel and all of the payments have been confirmed.

You check your sales figures then look at the news headlines as you sip your coffee. You run off an email to Codeaxa for an update on how your next store is coming along. You ponder your next big idea.

You ping a suicidal bird at a wooden tower of pigs and it collapses in a heap on the ground. You chuckle to yourself.

The day is your own while Volusion works slavishly. What will you do and where will you go?

About Codeaxa

Codeaxa is a Volusion specialist focusing on all aspects of customizing and custom coding the Volusion shopping cart platform, and most importantly, establishing long-term relationships with our clients. We have the deep seated desire to contribute to the successful goals of our clients.

Our most important goal is that we exceed our clients expectations at every opportunity. We will use every resource available to make certain this happens: expertise in design, software development, and marketing strategy. As long as we strive for that goal, we will continue building our history.

"We treat our customer right, take care of our people, be honest in our dealings, pass savings along to our customers, keep things simple, think smart, control costs and continuously improve operations".

We pass on our knowledge on in a practical and understandable format, this has achieved huge success for our customers and for us.

Our vast knowledge in e-commerce technologies brought about the development of Wealth-Creation-Online. This has been at the forefront of successful business building for our customers. Codeaxa has adopted a practical and easy to follow system for consumers who feel left out from the online business boom.

As customer's needs change, we will endeavor to maintain our leadership and to develop cutting-edge training products which are easy to implement. We will adopt a time-to-market policy so that customers are the first to take advantage of every new and successful development made by our team. This is Codeaxa's cutting-edge to competitive-edge strategy – First in the field so that you are first to benefit.

- **We can build you an amazing web site at an affordable price**
- **We can help with your SEO and marketing. Our results speak for themselves**
- **Our team of designers are some of the best in the industry**
- **We are the UK's leading Volusion specialist**
- **We have our own book published on internet business**
- **We sell our own products online so we practice what we preach.**

Made in United States
Orlando, FL
11 November 2026

90609396R00089